IN COURT IN LA PORTE

An Every-Name Index
—to the—
First Legal Proceedings
—in—
La Porte County Indiana
1833–1836

Including

Some Cases Heard
—in—
1837 and 1838

Compiled by

Harold Henderson

HERITAGE BOOKS
2013

HERITAGE BOOKS
AN IMPRINT OF HERITAGE BOOKS, INC.

Books, CDs, and more—Worldwide

For our listing of thousands of titles see our website
at
www.HeritageBooks.com

Published 2013 by
HERITAGE BOOKS, INC.
Publishing Division
100 Railroad Ave. #104
Westminster, Maryland 21157

Copyright © 2011 Harold Henderson
(midwestroots.net)

Cover map: "Township Maps, 2000," STATS Indiana Business Research Center at Indiana University's Kelley School of Business
(http://www.stats.indiana.edu/maptools/townships.asp: acessed 3 July 2011)

All rights reserved. No part of this book may be reproduced or transmitted in any form or by any means, electronic or mechanical, including photocopying, recording or by any information storage and retrieval system without written permission from the author, except for the inclusion of brief quotations in a review.

International Standard Book Numbers
Paperbound: 978-0-7884-5444-8
Clothbound: 978-0-7884-6957-2

INTRODUCTION

This book indexes all the persons, places, businesses, and institutions named in the earliest court records of La Porte County, Indiana, including more than 800 distinct surnames. The three handwritten books begin in 1833 -- the "minute record" of court procedures and rulings; the "complete record" of cases that went to trial; and the "judgment docket" of payments made.

Not enough genealogists use court records. This index should help researchers of all kinds identify and learn about the people who lived on the frontier more than 170 years ago.

The legal proceedings recorded in the books and indexed here describe fights, liquor sales, gambling parties, road building, timber cutting, slander, divorce, death, murder, and – above all – debt and the repayment of debt. Sometimes they state relationships. More often, they offer hints based on who put up money ("security" or "bail") to guarantee someone else's performance of a duty.

Caution! Always consult the original records before drawing genealogical conclusions. *This book is a road map to the records; it is not the records themselves.*

The original books indexed here are in the custody of the La Porte County Clerk:

CA = Complete Record A, June 1833 to April 1837, 595 pages, 11 x 15 inches, binding solid. Plaintiff index (loose) in front.

JA = Judgment Docket A, June 1833 to June 1838, 202 pages, 9 x 13 inches, good binding, occasional pages worn at the edges or faded ink. Index in rear, alphabetical by first letter of surname and then chronological.

MA = Minute Record A, June 1833 to October 1836, 537 pages, 9 x 13 inches, binding solid. Incomplete plaintiff index in front, alphabetical by first letter of surname and chronological within each letter.

Despite all efforts, this index may contain mistakes or misjudgments. Because some court cases in other jurisdictions were copied into these books, some names indexed refer to non-residents of La Porte County. Many jurisdictions changed as the population grew; New Durham Township, for instance, was much larger in 1833 than today.

The three books indexed here did not end at the same time. They are indexed together because each volume provides unique evidence about La Porte County, and contains names that do not appear in the other two; more than a dozen names beginning with "A" alone fall into this category. The complete record omits cases dismissed before trial, but provides the most details for those it does include. Thus the minute book names the individual accused of unlawfully selling liquor; the complete record usually adds the name of the alleged buyer and the price.

Not indexed here but important to researchers are the "loose papers" – the petitions, pleadings, receipts, summonses, and other materials filed with the court. Often they contain names and information not found in the books. They have been microfilmed and are listed in a typewritten binder in the clerk's office.

Spelling. Names are spelled as in the original, insofar as can be determined, regardless of correctness or consistency. The same person may be listed under several different spelling variants. In difficult cases I consulted other pages or the in-book index of plaintiffs, but no other sources. I have tried to err on the side of including many variants rather than assuming a common identity. Determining people's identities is not always simple, and it is a job for a genealogist, not an index.

Transcription. Common difficulties with the handwriting in these books include distinguishing between L and S; H, K, and R; M and N; m, n, u, e, and r; v and n; and e and i. An ambiguous first letter may cause a name to be indexed in an unexpected place -- be sure to think creatively and look at all possibilities. Troublesome readings are marked with a question mark. Alternative readings are in brackets or separated by a slash mark.

Numbering. A few pages in the original books were unnumbered or misnumbered. An unnumbered page following page X is called "X ½." If two pages bear the same number X, "X(2)" is used to refer to the second page. Some books begin or end with pages given no number. I have assigned them numbers in brackets [].

Coverage. All legible personal names are indexed, including those crossed out (so noted). All businesses, partnerships, and institutions are indexed, and the names of those involved are not always listed in the same order. Thus H. Wheeler is indexed last-name-first under W, but the business H. & T. Wheeler is indexed under H.

Court officials mentioned on almost every page – judges, clerks, prosecuting attorneys, and the sheriff -- are indexed only at their first appearance in a given term of court. Lesser officials, such as Justices of the Peace, bailiffs, constables, and attorneys, are indexed as regular people. Some individuals changed roles over time, and are indexed normally when appropriate.

Institutions and place names are indexed as well. Towns and townships not otherwise described are in La Porte County. Counties not otherwise described are in Indiana. Mentions of La Porte and Indiana appear on almost every page and are not indexed. "State of Indiana" as a party to a case appears very often and is not indexed.

Names indexed on a given page may appear more than once on that page. Cases involving one person may continue over more than one page. Jurors are indexed but not identified as such, as are attorneys who weren't frequently mentioned court officials.

Additional identifiers. Easily spotted identifiers of interest have been included, such as "spouse of," "estate," "naturalization," "divorce," and "deceased." Cases were not otherwise distinguished as to type, because much of that terminology is technical, obsolete, or both -- although in particular cases it may be important to understand the legalities. In addition:

"JP" refers to a justice of the peace, a lower level of township-based courts, few of whose records have survived. This notation will serve to locate cases where the JP record (no longer extant) was transcribed into the county record.

"Bail" refers to an individual who guaranteed (or was "security" or "surety" or "replevin bail" for) another person's payment of a fine, appearance in court, or performance of a duty. At this time and place, this can be genealogically significant.

"Sig" refers to what appears to be an individual's signature, based only on its being in a different hand from the regular scribe's. "Sig mark" refers to someone who signed by making a mark. "Admx" or "admr" refers to someone administering an estate (the designation implies that the deceased left no will). "Exec" refers to someone carrying out or executing a will.

"Et al." or "& c." mean "and others," meaning that other people not named in the title were involved in the case. Such cases are often complex and interesting. These people are usually named in the full case, so be sure to check the complete record and loose papers in these cases for more information.

Court session dates and pages. Court

IN COURT IN LA PORTE

was held in seasonal sessions or "terms." This index covers the entirety of each of the first books even though they vary in coverage. Business recorded between sessions was labeled "In Vacation."

In Complete Record A:
June Term 1833 begins CA:1
December Term 1833 CA:4
April Term 1834 CA:10
October Term 1834 CA:30
April Term 1835 CA:60
October Term 1835 CA:145
April Term 1836 CA:217
October Term 1836 CA:326
April Term 1837 CA:458

In Judgment Docket A:
June Term 1833 JA:1
December Term 1833 JA:1
April Term 1834 JA:2
October Term 1834 JA:5
April Term 1835 JA:10
October Term 1835 JA:23
April Term 1836 JA:34
October Term 1836 JA:56
April Term 1837 JA:78
October Term 1837 JA:106
April Term 1838 JA:134
June Term 1838 JA:163

In Minute Record A:
June Term 1833 begins on page MA:1
December Term 1833 MA:12
April Term 1834 MA:25
October Term 1834 MA:53
April Term 1835 MA:100
October Term 1835 MA:175
April Term 1836 MA:255
October Term 1836 MA:396

Acknowledgments. For advice and assistance, I thank the cordial employees of the county clerk, and fellow genealogists Dorothy Palmer, Fern Eddy Schultz, and other members of the La Porte County Genealogical Society. But nothing here is their fault.

Harold Henderson
July 2011

A

A Certain Indian CA:4, 20

A. & A. W. Harrison
  CA:188, 190, 191
  JA:32, 70, 71, 162
  MA:131

A. & S. W. Harrison JA:46

Abbot, William CA:26, 27

Abbott, William R. JA:126, 160, 171

Abney, Hezekiah CA:65

Ackerman, Jonathan
  CA:63, 66, 67
  MA:111

Adams, Isaac O.
  CA:29
  MA:55
Adams, Joseph MA:50
Adams, William
  CA:243
  JA:52, 120, 137, 158, 196
  MA:296
Adams, William bail CA:142, 143
Adams, William bail sig MA:160

Akins, Giles M. JA:142

Albany, New York CA:306, 307

Aldrich/Aldridge, Solomon
  CA:393
  JA:26
  MA:12, 25, 382, 442, 461, 485
Aldrich, Solomon sig JA:163
See also Alldrich, Auldrich

Alin, S.? CA:409

Alldrich, Solomon MA:193, 437, 455, 502, 503, 515
See also Aldrich/Aldridge, Auldrich

Allduck?, Solomon CA:335

Allegro, James CA:28

Allen & Steenbergen CA:534, 540-542
Allen, Alfred JA:118
Allen, George W.
   CA:204, 530, 531, 533-535, 541
   JA:31, 96, 98, 99, 103
   MA:194, 229, 526
Allen, George W. or G. W. sig JA:180
Allen, Nathan
   CA:57
   JA:108, 117
Allen, Nathan divorce
   CA:55, 56
   MA:6, 19, 22, 32, 88
Allen, Sylvia divorce
   CA:55, 56
   MA:6, 19, 22, 32, 88
Allen, Thomas JA:142
Allen, William
   CA:321
   JA:81, 116, 195
   MA:305, 382

Allison & Davis JA:42-44
Allison, J. F. MA:50(2), 72

Allison, John F. [crossed out] MA:83, 92, 216
Allison, John F.
  CA:39, 40, 48, 57-59, 61, 62,122-124, 126-128
  JA:10, 12, 13, 101
  MA:51, 58, 86, 93(2), 94, 96, 103, 113, 115,
  124, 157, 160, 221, 233, 236, 309(2), 322, 332, 339,
  488-490
Allison, W. MA:50(2)
Allison, William
  CA:39, 40, 57, 122-124
  MA:51, 93(2)
Allison, William deceased
  CA:58, 59, 127, 128
Allison, William deceased [crossed out] MA:83
Allison, William deceased MA:72, 86

Alsen, L. E. CA:323

Alvord, Fern C. JA:157

Alyea, Gideon JA:199

American Fur Company
  CA:25-27, 29
  JA:4
  MA:31, 40, 42, 43, 46, 48, 49

Anderson, David sig JA:149
Anderson, John JA:149
Anderson, Martin CA:30

Andrais, Lewis C. MA:503

Andrew/Andrews, A. P.
CA:323
MA:12, 220
Andrew/Andrews, Abraham P. [crossed out] MA:102
Andrew/Andrews, Abraham P. MA:95,108
Andrew, Abraham P. Jr. MA:476
Andrew/Andrews, Abram P.
CA:49, 240, 312
MA:44, 289, 351, 373, 383
Andrew/Andrews, James
CA:61, 62, 64-67, 173, 181, 192, 335, 337, 393, 405, 410, 415, 421, 427, 430
JA:97, 162
MA:9, 10, 50, 54, 213, 232, 382, 435, 437, 442, 455, 461, 480, 485, 492, 502, 503, 512, 515

Anthony, Charles JA:162

Anton, James naturalization sig MA:389

Archibald, James
CA:564-568
JA:74, 102
MA:503

Arcott, Ira JA:121
Arcott, Samuel JA:121

Armstrong, Elizabeth MA:476
Armstrong, James deceased MA:476
Armstrong, James heirs MA:476
Armstrong, William
  JA:6
  MA:168

Arnold, Isaac N. JA:138
Arnold, Isaac N. sig [inserted page] JA:138

Ashton, Eliakim
  CA:131, 188, 190-192
  JA:161, 183
  MA:131, 166, 205, 227, 232
Ashton, Eliakim bail CA:212
Ashton, Eliakim bail sig MA:195
Ashton, G. JA:165

Atkins, Jeremiah
  CA:553, 554
  JA:74, 77, 95
  MA:454, 501, 513
Atkins, Jeremiah T. JA:133, 148

Auldrich, Solomon CA:410, 421, 430
See Aldrich/Alldridge, Alldrich

Austin, Edward W. JA:135, 165

Averill, Charles K. ["Clark &" crossed out] JA:149

Averill, Charles K.
CA:572
JA:99, 179, 183, 196, 197, 202
Averill, Charles K. sig CA:132
Averill, Horatio JA:142

Avery, Dudley
CA:46
MA:50, 63, 73, 74
Avery, John L.
CA:42
JA:5
Avery, John S. MA:65, 67

Ayers, Frazee JA:107

B

Babcock, Amos JA:151

Bacon, N. JA:201
Bacon, Nathaniel JA:197

Baham/Bahan, Vincent MA:328, 443

Bailey Keeler & Remsen JA:124
Bailey, Alexis admr JA:121
Bailey, Joseph estate JA:121
Bailey, Mary admr JA:121

Bailly, Alexis JA:154, 174

Baily, John MA:12, 13

Baird & Ewing CA:192
Baird, Benjamin CA:568
Baird, Thomas D.
  CA:44, 195
  JA:8, 26
  MA:14, 29, 69, 417
Baird, Thos. S. CA:194

Baker, Alexis S. JA:166
Baker, Johnson & Co. JA:136
Baker, Marin MA:275
Baker, Martin
  CA:133, 225, 227, 230
  JA:174
  MA:2, 130, 167, 279, 284
Baker, Nathaniel JA:174
Baker, Samuel MA:167

Baldwin, Horace JA:170
Baldwin, John JA:109

Ball, H. CA:323
Ball, Harman
  CA:324, 495
  JA:78

Ball, Herman MA:461
Ball, Seneca CA:38-40, 46, 61-68, 173, 417
   JA:6, 128(2)
   MA:50, 54, 91, 205, 498
Ball, Seneca Dr. CA:397, 401, 402
Ball, Willard
   CA:337, 421
   MA:502, 503
Ball, William
   CA:139
   MA:435

Ballard, C. A. constable MA:164
Ballard, Christopher A. MA:100
Ballard, Christopher A. bailiff MA:162

Ballone, Christopher A. MA:167

Bank of Michigan CA:318, 509
Bank of River Raisin, President & directors MA:114
Bank of the Metropolis CA:204, 205
Bank of the United States at Cincinnati CA:118, 119, 198
Bank of the United States CA:120, 121

Banks, James
   CA:403
   JA:71
   MA:480
Barber, Horace CA:203

Barger, Samuel
   CA:209, 286, 296, 297
   JA:40
   MA:28

Barker, Horace CA:323
Barker, John JA:110-112, 122, 177
Barker, L. CA:321
Barker, O. H. bail JA:201
Barker, Oscar A. bail CA:569
Barker, Oscar A. JA:92, 167, 169
Barker, S. CA:286
Barker, Samuel
   CA:225, 230, 240, 265, 277, 282, 302, 312, 317, 322
   MA:275, 284, 322, 335, 351, 354, 355, 359, 365-367, 373

Barnes, George JA:199
Barnes/Barns, George W. MA:87, 328, 382
Barnes/Barns, George W. divorce [crossed out] MA:78
Barnes/Barns, George W. divorce MA:158, 217, 425
Barnes, James R.
   CA:502, 503, 570, 571
   JA:84, 89
Barnes/Barns, Lucinda MA:87, 328
Barnes/Barns, Lucinda divorce [crossed out] MA:78
Barnes/Barns, Lucinda divorce MA:158, 217, 425

Barnett, John JA:110

Barns, Elijah JA:127

Barratt, Jacob
  CA:405
  MA:480

Bartholomew, Jeremiah
  CA:10, 52, 104, 193, 196, 197
  JA:2, 9, 11, 26, 29, 39, 65, 75
  MA:25, 81, 106, 116, 120, 193, 215, 250, 308, 316, 447, 455
Bartholomew, Jeremiah divorce MA:367, 506
Bartholomew, Joseph
  CA:47, 263, 264
  JA:47
  MA:324, 354
Bartholomew, Rebecca JA:75
Bartholomew, Rebecca divorce MA:367, 506

Barton, Luke W. MA:164

Bass, Jacob W. JA:119
Bass, James CA:321
Bass, John M. MA:335

Bassett, Horace JA:73

Bauerly, Sidney S. JA:148

Baugham, Vincent MA:383

Baxter, Allen
   JA:37
   MA:217, 292

Bay & Liston MA:7, 8

Bay, John M.
   CA:225, 227, 230
   MA:50, 167, 275, 279, 284, 322

Bayer, Samuel MA:313

Bear, Isaac
   CA:414, 460, 462, 463
   MA:396
Bear, Isaac et al. JA:146

Beard, Benjamin CA:467
Beard, Benjamin bail CA:462

Bearne, Patrick MA:113
See also Berine, Bierne, Birne, Burne, Burnes, Burns

Beaubien, Mark JA:91, 184

Beckman, John CA:529

Beckner, John
  CA:467, 494, 541, 558, 568, 583
  MA:383

Beckwith, E. A. sig JA:152
Beckwith, Elijah A. JA:170

Beers, Joseph D. JA:123

Behan/Baham, Luke naturalization MA:304

Belden, John
  JA:67
  MA:461

Beldings, Solomon MA:511

Beliles, John MA:447

Bell, Reason MA:525
Bell, Resin CA:221, 222, 224, 226, 228, 234, 332
Bell, Rezin
  CA:177, 182-184, 186, 187
  MA:166, 175

Belshaw, George
  CA:589, 590
  JA:96

Benedict & Wetmore
  JA:43
  MA:124

Benedict, Charles A. MA:124, 233, 332, 339

Benjamin, Calvin MA:161

Bennett, Hiram MA:185, 260

Benson, Samuel bail JA:119

Bentley, Rensalaer JA:168
Bentley/Bently, Thomas
   CA:409, 410, 414, 460, 462-464, 529
   JA:72, 188
   MA:396, 485, 486, 526

Benton, Royal
   CA:553, 554
   JA:74, 77, 95
   MA:501, 513
Benton, Rozal MA:454

Berget, Silas JA:160

Berine/Beirne Patrick MA:288
See also Bearne, Bierne, Birne, Burne, Burnes, Burns

Bernard, William H.
   CA:412, 413
   JA:69
   MA:470

Bias, Garret/Garrett
    CA:201, 495
    JA:30, 90, 119, 197, 198
    MA:223
Bias, Garret bail CA:592

Bickner, John CA:461, 462, 464, 563

Bierne & Duffy
    CA:492
    JA:94
Bierne, Patrick CA:492
See also Bearne, Berine, Birne, Burne, Burnes, Burns

Bigelow, Abijah JA:145
Bigelow, Abijah bail JA:146
Bigelow, Increase S. JA:191
Bigelow/Biglow, Jacob
    JA:111, 112, 146
    MA:382

Bikies, Jno. CA:197

Billings, Michael MA:271
Billings, Michael A. MA:400

Billips, Edward
    CA:287, 288
    JA:45
    MA:345

Billips, Edward [crossed out] MA:342

Binford, William
   CA:194, 195
   MA:194

Bingham, Benjamin
   JA:41
   MA:319
Bingham, William
   JA:41
   MA:319

Birch, Calvin MA:107
Birch, David MA:107
Birch, Ira CA:229, 260

Bird?, William Jr. MA:491

Birne, Patrick MA:238
See also Bearne, Berine, Bierne, Burne, Burnes, Burns

Bishop, Elijah MA:166
Bishop, George
   CA:69, 71, 75, 80, 93-96, 100, 102
   MA:189, 264, 399

Black, James
   CA:46, 49, 54, 414, 460, 462
   MA:50, 63, 73, 80, 84, 90, 396

Black, James sig JA:201
Black, Nathaniel JA:201
Black, Ward
  CA:233
  MA:112

Blackburn, A. CA:34-37
Blackburn, Alex CA:141 page attached
Blackburn, Alexander MA:12, 25, 166

Blair & Adams JA:158
Blair Adams & Currin JA:176
Blair, C. B. JA:202
Blair, C. R. CA:131
Blair, Chauncy B. or C. B. sig JA:130
Blair, James
  CA:61, 63-67, 173
  MA:12, 50, 54
Blair, Jane JA:102
Blair, Jane divorce MA:510
Blair, John JA:102, 137, 158, 196
Blair, John divorce MA:510

Blake, David A.
  CA:181-183
  JA:31
  MA:216, 228

Blake, Isaac
  CA:35, 36, 180
  JA:7, 8
  MA:52, 61, 74, 78, 185, 190, 260, 265, 397, 399
Blake, Isaac bail
  CA:37
  MA:64
Blake, J.
  JA:29
  MA:26
Blake, Joseph [crossed out] JA:52
Blake, Joseph
  CA:25, 26, 28, 46, 50, 63, 80-82, 234, 244, 332
  JA:4, 5, 7, 10, 17, 32, 56
  MA:22, 31, 40, 43, 46, 48, 56, 57, 60-63, 66, 67, 71, 81, 101, 135, 142, 143, 164, 218, 219, 277, 297, 311, 401, 402, 412, 463, 527
Blake, Joseph bail
  CA:61, 69-74, 87-91, 100-103, 134, 182, 185
  MA:102, 228, 232, 416
Blake, Joseph bail sig MA:104, 132, 136-138, 145-147, 151-153
Blake, Joseph bailiff MA:162
Blake, Joseph constable
  CA:143, 201, 203, 259
  MA:164, 165
Blake, Theophilus MA:167
Blake, W. MA:171
Blake, W. D. MA:26

Blake, Ward [CA:0 – apparently a misplaced page from April 1835]
Blake, Ward [crossed out] MA:87Blake, Ward
    CA:24-28, 37, 46, 50, 68-74, 81, 125, 126, 133, 203, 323, 331, 335, 421, 431
        JA:4, 5, 7, 10, 13, 15, 16, 37, 56, 57, 65, 76, 150, 180
        MA:12, 22, 28, 29, 31, 35, 40, 42, 43, 46, 48, 54, 56, 57, 62-64, 66, 71, 79, 81, 90, 94, 115, 119, 130, 132, 136-138, 171, 250, 293, 311, 401, 402, 412, 415, 437, 456, 463, 502, 513, 527
Blake, Ward bail
    CA:36, 80, 83, 132
    JA:14
    MA:61, 142, 143
Blake, Ward bail sig MA:121
Blake, Ward et al. JA:12, 40
Blake, Ward D.
    CA:244-246
    JA:52
    MA:297
Blake, William
    CA:25, 26, 28, 150, 180
    JA:4
    MA:31, 40, 43, 46, 48, 71, 79, 112, 180, 188, 189, 264, 398, 399

Blaylock CA:559
Blaylock, Hannah CA:559

Blaylock, John
  CA:559 JA:86
  MA:505

Blevin, Robert C. MA:119, 129

Bliven, R. C. JA:15

Blodget, E. B. CA:352, 355
Blodget, Elijah B.
  CA:350-354, 356
  JA:54
  MA:244(2), 245, 246, 309, 315, 440, 441
Blodget, Tyler K.
  CA:350-354
  JA:54
  MA:244(2), 245, 246, 440, 441
Blodget, Tyler R. MA:309

Bloomington, Monroe County MA:168

Blydenburg, R. F. JA:180

Blythe, Benjamin J. JA:194-195

Board of Commissioners of La Porte County
  CA:543, 545
  MA:325, 455

Boardman, William E. JA:119
Boarst/Borst, William M.
  CA:427
  JA:120
  MA:512

Bog/Bogg/Boggs, James
  CA:36, 37
  MA:27, 33, 39

Bolls, Eliakim JA:137

Bond, Abner D.
  CA:251
  JA:53
  MA:300, 384
Bond, D. Y. CA:193
Bond, Jesse
  CA:174, 181, 182, 184, 192
  MA:166, 205, 208, 213, 220, 228, 232
Bond, John
  CA:46, 51, 174, 181, 182, 184, 192
  JA:9
  MA:82, 166, 205, 208, 213, 220, 228, 232
Bond, John bail CA:270
Bond, John bail sig MA:350
Bond, William
  CA:468
  JA:80

Bond, William Jr.   CA:297, 469
    MA:28, 50, 382

Born, D. J. CA:194

Bosgars, W.? CA:321

Boswell, Ezra MA:169

Bowell, John MA:167

Bowen [Brown crossed out] JA:101
Bowen, James
    CA:317
    MA:359
Bowen, John
    CA:323
    JA:104

Bowers, James JA:111

Bown, James MA:503

Boyd, Daniel MA:123

Bradet, John MA:13

Bradley & Fletcher JA:158
Bradley & Jurnegan CA:539, 540

Bradley, Bartholomew JA:148
Bradley, Henry JA:120, 158Bradley, J. H. CA:544
Bradley, John A. MA:500
Bradley, John H. [crossed out] MA:325
Bradley/Bradly, John H.
   CA:237, 238, 283, 284, 305, 313, 314, 397, 402, 420, 422, 425, 516-518, 525, 527, 530, 531, 533, 534, 543, 564, 567, 575-577, 591, 592
    JA:35, 54, 71, 83, 114, 119, 162, 197
    MA:196, 380, 383, 419, 460, 476, 515, 526
Bradley/Bradly, John H. sig JA:83, 84, 97, 149, 150, 152, 172
Bradley, Leverett bail JA:154

Brand, Michael
  CA:495
  MA:50, 382, 491

Branson, David
  CA:62, 137, 141, 144, 557
  MA:50, 103, 122, 129, 132, 159, 161
Branson, David constable CA:278

Brayton, Russel C.
  JA:53
  MA:320
Brayton, Stephen
  CA:217, 219, 220
  JA:34
  MA:203, 204, 256-259

Brewster, J. JA:149
Brewster, L. JA:149

Briggs, Ira
  JA:10
  MA:31, 42, 44, 53, 93

Brison, William JA:26

Broaded, John
  CA:417
  MA:12, 498

Brooke, Henry L. JA:191

Broom, Andrew M.
  CA:44, 45
  JA:8
  MA:69

Brown & Haas
  CA:524
  JA:85
Brown, C. W.
  CA:232, 326, 328, 329, 331, 334, 336, 338, 340, 342, 458, 459, 465
  MA:251, 255
Brown, C. W., constable CA:201

Brown, Chapel W.
 CA:116, 137, 144, 185, 192, 281, 532, 541, 557, 568
 MA:12, 13, 50, 122, 128, 129, 132, 161, 229, 232, 365, 367, 516
Brown, Chapel W. bail
 CA:466
 MA:514
Brown, Chapel W. or C. W. sig JA:103
Brown, Chappel W. bailiff MA:396
Brown, Daniel
 CA:61, 63-67, 173, 511, 512, 524
 JA:85
 MA:50, 54
Brown, Daniel sig JA:177
Brown, David MA:433
Brown, Elijah
 CA:86, 89, 101
 MA:14
Brown, Elijah A. JP MA:168
Brown, Elijah H.
 CA:1, 68, 70-85, 88, 90-100, 102-112, 145, 146, 148-151, 153-157, 159-166, 168, 169, 171, 172, 175, 176, 178, 179, 217, 219, 229, 231
 MA:12, 25, 100
Brown, Elijah H. JP CA:140-142, 200, 211, 239
Brown, Emory A. MA:2, 95
Brown, Ezekiel CA:464

Brown, John
  CA:11, 93-99, 265, 337, 541
  JA:18, 19, 50, 51, 86, 101, 128(2), 134, 157, 161, 172, 187, 192, 194   MA:148-151, 295, 311, 377, 436, 526
Brown, John bail
  CA:431
  JA:2
  MA:26
Brown, John bail sig MA:515
Brown, John sig JA:87, 140, 143, 178, 193
Brown, Joseph M.
  CA:594
  JA:81
Brown, William CA:409

Bryant, Jacob
  CA:345
  JA:59
  MA:426
Bryant, Josiah MA:2, 12, 18, 507

Bryson, Abraham A. admr. &c. JA:175
Bryson, Abraham A. JA:110
Bryson, Samuel deceased JA:110

Buck/Burk, Warren L. CA:385
See also Burke, Burch, Burke

Buel, George C. CA:24, 48
Buel, J.M. constable CA:129, 130
Buel, James JA:79

Buel, James M. [crossed out] MA:429
Buel, James M.
  CA:139, 473-475 MA:78, 89, 274, 431
Buel, James M. bail CA:471
Buel, James M. bailiff MA:91, 96
Buel, James M. constable CA:24, 29, 31, 32, 41, 51
Buel, James M. sworn officer MA:54

Buell, James M. et al. JA:9

Buffalo & Mississippi Rail Road Company JA:189
Buffalo, New York CA:188-193

Bulla, William
  CA:305
  MA:305
Bulla, William Sr.
  CA:303
  JA:44
  MA:336, 386

Bunce, Simon G. MA:50

Bunch, Ira [crossed out] MA:203

Bunyan, Elizabeth
  JA:71
  MA:482

Burch, Admiral MA:166
Burch, Admiral bail MA:215

Burch, Admiral or A. sig JA:110
Burch, Calvin MA:50
Burch, Harry MA:291
Burch, Henry MA:214
Burch, Henry bail MA:209
Burch, Ira
    CA:230, 260
    MA:205(2), 209, 214, 283, 291, 347
Burch, Ira et al. MA:225
Burch, Warren MA:214, 291
See also Buck, Burke, Burch

Burgess, Austin MA:446

Burk/Burke, Warren/Warran L.
    CA:393
    JA:59, 70
    MA:306, 331, 428, 442, 443, 475
See also Buck, Burch, Burch

Burleigh, Richard JA:122

Burlingame, Abel
    CA:61, 62, 64-67, 173, 265, 282-284, 302, 397, 401, 402, 469
    JA:49, 80
    MA:50, 54, 331, 335, 354, 382, 491

Burlingame, Abel sig MA:362

Burne, Patrick MA:192
See also Bearne, Berine, Bierne, Birne, Burns, Burnes

Burner, Abraham MA:516

Burnes, Abraham bailiff MA:396
See also Bearne, Berine, Bierne, Birne, Burne, Burns

Burns & Duffy MA:437
Burns, Christopher
  CA:166, 167, 177, 280, 282
  JA:27, 29, 50
  MA:201, 213, 328,367
Burns, George W. divorce MA:33
Burns, Lucinda divorce MA:33
Burns, Patrick MA:72, 437
See also Bearne, Berine, Bierne, Birne, Burne

Burnside, Andrew
  CA:68, 70-86, 88-112, 145, 146, 148-151, 153-159, 160-166, 168, 169, 171, 172, 175, 176, 178, 179, 217, 219, 229, 231, 428, 430
  JA:12, 76, 90, 112, 169
  MA:12, 50, 71, 100, 174, 254, 295, 305, 504, 515
Burnside, Andrew bail CA:243, 317, 568
Burnside, Andrew bail sig MA:296, 359
Burnside, Andrew treasurer La Porte County MA:79, 112

Burr & Johnson JA:151
Burr, D. JA:169

Burr, David [crossed out] JA:127
Burr, David bail JA:118, 126, 127, 144, 164, 173
Burr, David   CA:171, 502, 503, 505, 506, 516, 520
   JA: 60, 71, 84, 87-89, 122, 128(2), 130, 170, 172, 178, 185, 189, 191-193
   MA:320, 338, 385, 406, 441, 462, 583
Burr, David et al. JA:187
Burr, Horace
   CA:462
   JA:185, 193
Burr, Jona. JA:130
Burr, Jonas sig JA:191
Burr, Jonathan JA:155, 178
Burr, Jonathan & other JA:155

Burrows, James
   CA:318
   JA:42
   MA:324, 329

Buss, John M. CA:302

Bussey/Bussy, Hezekiah
   CA:61, 63, 64, 66, 67, 173
   MA:50, 54

Butler, Joel
   CA:225, 230, 277, 282, 287, 302, 317
   MA:167, 275, 279, 283, 322, 335, 346, 359, 365-367
Butler, John CA:227

IN COURT IN LA PORTE

Butts, James
    CA:185   MA:277, 400

C

C. Donaldson & Co. CA:198, 429

Cabell, Landon R.
   JA:39
   MA:308

Cadwalader/Cadwalder, Cadwallader, Amos
   CA:46, 49, 54
   MA:50, 73, 84, 90
Cadwalader, Byron MA:382

Caldwell, James bail JA:11

Caldwell, James sig mark MA:110
Caldwell, Oliver S. MA:109
Caldwell, Oliver V. CA:118

Callen, Jacob MA:525

Calison, James sig JA:46

Callison, James CA:285

Calvin, Dewit L. MA:194

Campbell, Charles MA:12, 13
Campbell, Margaret MA:372, 487
Campbell, T. A. E. CA:288
Campbell, Thomas A. E.
   CA:436-445
   JA:58
   MA:197-200, 265-267, 423-425
Campbell, William
   CA:17, 132, 133, 144, 407, 408
   JA:15, 39, 73, 184, 192
   MA:44, 119, 130, 161, 310, 461, 483, 487, 490
Campbell, William sig MA:132
Campbell, William, Margaret's husband MA:372

Canal Telegraph MA:93 (2)

Canby, J. T. bail JA:164

Cannon, G. W. CA:344
Cannon, George W.
  CA:343
  JA:57
  MA:416

Carlus Jacob H. JA:194

Carmac, William
  CA:141
  MA:128, 159, 161
  See also Carmack, Cormac, Cormack

Carmack, Abram JA:114
Carmack, William
  CA:144, 557
  JA:114
  MA:50, 103, 122, 129
Carmack, William bail JA:140
  See also Carmac, Cormac, Cormack

Carpenter, Charles W. JA:136
Carpenter, Henry
  MA:4, 12, 25, 167

Carter & Barker JA:122, 145
Carter, Henry C. JA:123
Carter, J. S. sig JA:122
Carter, Jacob JA:110

Carter, Jacob S.
  JA:111, 112, 177, 200
Carter, John MA:2

Carver, David JA:183

Cass County
  CA:207
  MA:93(2), 111, 126
Cass, Lew Secretary of War MA:123

Cassaday, William MA:184

Casteel, Elijah JA:136
Casteel, Elijah bail CA:195, 196
Casteel, Elijah bail sig MA:194
Casteel, Elijah constable CA:53
Casteel, William MA:318

Castle CA:277
Castle, _____ MA:366

Cathcart, C. W. CA:382
Cathcart, Cha. W. JP CA:23
Cathcart, Charles bail CA:200
Cathcart, Charles W.
  CA:116, 141, 144, 557
  MA:50, 122, 128, 129, 159, 161
Cathcart, James
  JA:23
  MA:178, 180

Cathcart, James L.
  CA:150, 200
  JA:30
  MA:222
Cathcart, James L. Junr. CA:200
Cathcart, John CA:201
Cathcart, John bail sig MA:223

Catlin, J. JA:57
Catlin, Nicholas M. JA:133
Catlin, Theodore
  CA:185
  MA:229

Cator, Hiram JA:141
Cator, William CA:321

Cattrell, Samuel L. sheriff St. Joseph County MA:173

Cattron, Valentine sig JA:190

Caulkins & Darrow JA:149

Center/Centre Township
  CA:29, 31, 32, 41, 138, 244(2), 245, 350, 353
  MA:246

Chace, William C. CA:312, 377
See also Chase

Chamberlain & Caldwell
  CA:118, 120, 121
  JA:11
  MA:109
Chamberlain, Ebenezer M. MA:104
Chamberlain, J. W. bail CA:131
Chamberlain, James L.
  CA:118, 121
  MA:109
Chamberlain, Joseph W. JA:116, 118, 126

Chamberlin, Levi constable CA:264

Champman, Samuel E. JA:73

Chandler, Moses JA:199

Chandonais, John Bts. MA:89

Chandonnois, Jean Baptiste MA:52
See also Shandonnois

Chapman, G. E. CA:232
Chapman, J. B. CA:27
Chapman, Jared [crossed out] JA:7, 8
Chapman, Jared
  CA:6, 7, 42, 47, 587, 591, 592
  JA:1, 5, 78, 98, 150
  MA:17, 19, 65, 67, 69, 75
Chapman, Jared admr JA:94

Chapman, Jared bail
 CA:35
 JA:119, 181
 MA:58
Chapman, John B.
 CA:56, 60
 JA:176
 MA:2, 49 1/2
Chapman, John B. prosecutor
 CA:4
 MA:4, 5, 14, 26
Chapman, John
 CA:174, 232, 283, 326, 327, 329, 331, 334, 336, 338, 340, 342, 458, 459, 465
 JA:120
 MA:166, 208, 255
Chapman, Joseph bail
 CA:42, 282-284
 JA:49, 120
 MA:67, 331, 362, 382
Chapman, S. E.
 CA:286, 323, 326, 328, 329, 331, 334, 336, 338, 340, 342, 458, 459, 465
 MA:255
Chapman, Samuel CA:460
Chapman, Samuel C.
 CA:414
 MA:382

Chapman, Samuel E.
　CA:67, 407, 417, 462, 463
　JA:67
　MA:383, 396, 462, 483, 490, 498
Chapman, Samuel E. bail
　CA:362
　MA:449
Chapman, Thomas sig JA:176

Charles, Abraham CA:317
　MA:167, 359, 365
Charles, Abram
　CA:282
　MA:12, 364, 367
Charles, Abram bail
　CA:358
　MA:448

Chase, H. CA:196
Chase, Henry MA:25
Chase, William C.
　CA:265, 375, 376, 460
　JA:66, 118, 156
　MA:354, 363, 373, 457, 459, 476, 505
Chase, William
　CA:227, 374
　MA:279
See also Chace

Cheney, John JA:135

Cheney, Solomon CA:132
 JA:191

Chicago CA:515, 519

Chinn, C. JA:15
Chinn, Chichester
  CA:68, 70-86, 88-112, 145, 146, 148-151, 153-158, 160-166, 168-172, 175, 176, 178, 179, 217, 219, 229, 231
  MA:50, 100, 119, 129

Chittenden & Lamson JA:168, 177
Chittenden, Austin
  CA:522, 523
  JA:89, 117, 123, 124, 128(2), 155, 194

Chumm, T. R. CA:418

Churchill, Timothy JA:137
Churchill, Wm. E. JA:137

Cincinnati CA:113, 120, 121, 198, 418

Cisnee, John
  CA:232, 458, 459, 465
  MA:255

Cisney, John MA:166

Cisney, Robert
  CA:330
  MA:436

Cissal/Cissall/Cissel/Cissell, John CA:327, 329, 331, 334, 336, 338, 340, 342

Cisswell, John CA:326

Clark & Averill
  CA:572
  JA:99
Clark & Fravel JA:159
Clark County, Ohio CA:486, 488, 490, 491
Clark, Alden
  CA:132, 572
  JA:99, 138, 196, 197
  MA:250, 294
Clark, Amzi
  CA:409
  MA:166, 480, 485
Clark, David JA:164
Clark/Clarke, John
  CA:461, 464, 495, 529, 541, 558, 568, 583
  MA:383
Clark, Jonas JA:130, 140, 147, 148, 164, 166, 167
Clark, Richard
  JA:39, 45
  MA:308, 341
Clark, Staats JA:181

Clark, William
  CA:1, 13, 14, 232, 233, 326-331, 334, 336, 338-340, 342, 458, 459, 465, 563
  MA:27, 34, 38, 42, 43, 167, 255, 372, 476
Clark, William county surveyor MA:161
Clark, William sen.? MA:12
Clark/Clarke, William S.
  CA:506, 507, 546, 547, 549-552
  JA:51, 73, 191
  MA:253, 294, 382, 491, 507
Clark, William S. or W. S. sig JA:85, 98
Clark, Wm S. bail JA:130

Clarkson, John [on inserted paper] JA:123
Clarkson, John M.
  CA:363, 364
  JA:64, 113, 123, 449, 450

Clauson, Oliver
  CA:174, 181, 182, 184, 428
  MA:166, 205, 208, 213, 220, 228, 504, 515
  See also Closser, Clossen, Closson

Clayburn, Henry MA:47
See also Clyburn

Cleft, Hiram MA:441
See also Clift

Clement, William
 CA:240, 265, 286, 302, 312, 322, 374-376, 409
 JA:66, 114
 MA:50, 167, 289, 335, 351, 354, 355, 373, 457, 485
Clement, William bail
 CA:138, 377, 412
 MA:486
Clement, William bail sig MA:134, 459

Clerk of the District Court W. D. for District of Indiana JA:73

Clift, Hiram
 JA:87
 MA:320, 338
See also Cleft

Cline, George MA:50, 166
Cline, George JP CA:264, 288
Cline, John
 CA:46, 49, 54
 MA:50, 63, 73, 80, 84, 90

Clinger, George CA:532
Clinger, George, constable CA:193
See also Olinger

Clossen, Daniel MA:302
Clossen, Oliver JA:76, 90
See also Clauson/Clawson, Closser, Closson

Closser, Nicholas W.
　CA:461, 462, 464, 494, 541, 558, 563, 568, 583
　MA:383
Closser, Nicholas W. bail CA:325
Closser, Nicholas W. bail sig MA:355
See also Clossen, Closson

Closson, Oliver
　CA:430
　MA:28
See also Clossen, Closser

Clum?, George JA:45

Clybourn JA:166, 167

Clybourne, Archibald JA:130

Clyburn, Henly/Henley
　CA:23, 68, 70-86, 88-112, 145, 146, 148-151, 153-166, 168, 169, 171, 172, 175-179, 217, 219, 229, 231
　JA:4
　MA:12, 50, 100
See also Clayburn

Cobb, John P.
　JA:41
　MA:319

Cobb, Whitman
   JA:49
   MA:316, 351, 361 See also Colb

Coble CA:321

Cochran, John
   CA:173, 174
   JA:33
   MA:106, 208

Colb, Whitman JP CA:278, 279
See also Cobb

Cole & Peck JA:128
Cole Peck & Co. JA:153, 154
Cole Peck & Co. bail JA:146
Cole, Jacob CA:332
Cole, John CA:48
Cole, John W.
   CA:414, 460, 462, 463
   MA:12, 382, 396
Cole, Warren
   CA:131
   JA:144, 168
Cole, Warren bail JA:174

Coleman, Jacob [crossed out] MA:6

Coleman, Jacob
  CA:3, 133, 141, 144, 177, 182-184, 187, 221, 223, 224, 226, 228, 234, 349
  JA:1, 32, 34, 61   MA:2-4, 8, 12, 19, 130, 159, 161, 175, 237, 256-258, 312, 439
Coleman, Jacob bail
  CA:174
  MA:204, 208
Coleman, John
  CA:105-107
  JA:20
  MA:154, 155
See also Colman

Colerick, D. V. MA:136
Colerick, David H.
  CA:85, 86
  MA:2

Collamer, Danvers G. JA:136

Collins, Harvey JA:146
Collins, Harvey et al. JA:172
Collins, J. W. constable CA:573
Collins, Joshua W.
  MA:527
  JA:90

Collison, James
  CA:139
  MA:346

Colman, Jacob MA:8
See also Coleman

Columbia County, Pennsylvania CA:528

Colver, Dewit L. or S.
   CA:68, 70-86, 89-112, 145, 146, 148-151, 153-157, 159-166, 168, 169, 171, 172, 175, 176-178, 182-184, 186, 187, 217, 219, 221, 222, 224, 226, 228, 229, 231, 234, 332
   MA:175
Colver, Dewitt L. bailiff MA:255
See also Culver

Colvin, David L. MA:378

Combs & Parker JA:48
Combs, Joseph P.
   CA:321, 323
   JA:48
   MA:354, 355
Combs, Robert JA:153

Comer, Lewis
   JA:62
   MA:328, 383, 443

Commissioners of Laporte County JA:82

Comparet & Coquillard   CA:25   JA:4
   MA:42, 46, 48
Comparet, Alexis MA:48
Comparet, Francis
   CA:25-27, 29
   JA:4
   MA:31, 43, 46, 48, 49

Comparit, F. MA:40

Conden, Reynolds sig JA:200

Cone, A. G. MA:12
Cone, G. A. CA:119
Cone, Gustavus A.
   CA:11, 118, 120, 121
   JA:11
   MA:13, 109, 166

Congdon, James
   JA:128, 151

Conklin, Aaron JA:134

Cook, Levi JA:155

Cooper, H. MA:18

Cooper, Henry
   CA:8, 212, 21
   MA:14

Coquillard, A. MA:40
Coquillard, Alex/Alexis
   CA:25-27, 29, 204
   JA:4, 31
   MA:31, 43, 46, 49, 194, 229

Cord, George M. MA:50

Coreless/Coreliss, Isaac CA:221, 222, 224, 226, 228, 234, 332
See also Corlis, Corliss

Corey, Aylmer J. JA:166

Corithe/Couthe?, James C. CA:141 page attached

Corliss, Isaac
   CA:177, 182-184, 186,187
   MA:166, 175
Corliss, Isaac sig JA:148
Corliss, Jeremiah JA:115, 148
See also Coreless/Coreliss

Cormac, William CA:116
See also Carmac, Carmack, Cormack

Cormack, William CA:62
See also Carmac, Carmack, Cormac

Cornwall/Cornwell/Cornwelle/Cornwill, Thomas
CA:227, 230, 265, 282, 287, 302, 312, 317, 322
MA:279, 284, 322, 335, 346, 351, 354, 355, 359, 365-367, 373

Cory, Aylmer J. bail CA:529

Corydon MA:123

Cosser, Nicholas W. CA:529

Cottom, John JA:151

Coulter, James JA:115

County Jail MA:240, 343

Cowden, Reynolds JA:122, 159

Cowns, David associate judge MA:53

Cox, Samuel
CA:276, 336, 337
JA:40, 41, 49, 50
MA:160, 167, 173, 317, 318, 362, 363, 366

Cox, William First Burgess MA:170

Crandall, Horatio JA:152
Crandall, Horatio A. JA:75
Crandall, Horatio N. MA:504Crandall, John E. CA: 225
Crandall, John I./J. [crossed out] MA:336
Crandall, John I./J.
  CA:227, 230, 265, 277, 282, 302, 312, 317, 322
  JA:161
  MA:50(2), 167, 279, 284, 322, 335, 351, 354, 355, 359, 365-367, 373
Crandall, John S. MA:275

Craninia?, Richard CA:141 page attached

Crawford, David
  CA:137, 240
  MA:50, 132, 289, 302
Crawford, William bail JA:138

Crawfordsville CA:194

Creekpann, William MA:361

Creekpaum & Collison JA:46
Creekpaum, W. bail JA:34

Creekpaum, William
  CA:78, 90, 285, 336, 337
  JA:109
  MA:141, 310, 318, 346, 363

Creekpaum, William bail
CA:227
MA:281
Creekpaum, William sig MA:346 [paper pasted in]

Creekpaun, William CA:79, 89

Creekpawm, William
CA:323, 324, 335
JA:41, 46

Creekpawn, William
CA:209
JA:17

Crogswell, Joseph [crossed out] JA:111

Cromwell, Thomas MA:167

Crook JA:77

Crooks/Crook, William B.
CA:553, 554
JA:74

MA:454, 501

Crosier, Aaron MA:243

Cross, Mordecai [crossed out] MA:454

Cross, Mordecai
   CA:185, 226, 357, 358, 422-424, 451-453, 475, 476
   JA:60, 63, 68, 75, 143, 182, 196
   MA:229, 293, 371, 408, 409, 418, 421, 432, 433, 447, 448, 466, 467, 508, 518
Cross, Mordecai bail
   CA:181   JA:31
   MA:227, 369

Crumbecker, John JA:178

Culver, A. L. CA:409
Culver, Dewit L. MA:100
See also Colver

Curtis, James B. JA:116
Curtis, Joseph
   JA:26
   MA:193

Cutler, L. JA:13, 14
Cutler, Leonard
   CA:131, 271-275, 457
   JA:37, 189
   MA:12, 25, 116, 195, 289, 292, 333, 382, 387, 388, 419, 509
Cutler, Leonard bail JA:174
Cutler, Leonard sig JA:43

Cutter, Leonard MA:116, 121, 216, 226

D

D. & N. W. Low
  CA:511, 512
  JA:151, 190

Daily, Daniel JA:29

Dann, Jesse CA:309
Dann, Jesse C.
  CA:306, 308
  MA:294

Darland, Silas
 CA:62, 63, 66
 JA:11
 MA:104, 187, 188

Darlington, Samuel JA:142, 165, 180, 182

Davis, Caleb B. MA:50
Davis, Handy JA:116
Davis, Harry MA:437
Davis, Henry [crossed out] MA:216
Davis, Henry & c. MA:309(2), 322, 332, 339
Davis, Henry
 CA:132, 134-138, 151-160, 337, 350-356, 410, 556-559
 JA:15, 23, 24, 36, 82 101
 MA:32, 117, 122, 124, 126, 130-132, 134, 162, 180-183, 221, 233, 234, 236, 244(2), 245, 246, 288, 309, 315, 323, 339, 436, 440, 441, 485, 488-490
Davis, Henry sig mark JA:54
Davis, John C. JA:162
Davis, John C. admr et al. JA:156
Davis, John T. CA:528
Davis, Joseph JA:85
Davis, N. CA:209
Davis, Nathanial/Nathaniel
 CA:38, 39, 209
 JA:10, 40
 MA:92, 311
Davis, William H. MA:487

Dawson, Matthias MA:50

Day, Lovila A. JA:162
Day, Peter
 CA:221-223, 323, 340, 459, 463, 573
 JA:34, 61, 97
 MA:267, 407, 434

Dean, Jonathan M. JA:201

Dearborn County
 CA:9
 MA:22

Deats/Drats, Cuyler
 JA:39
 MA:307

Decker, Michael CA:532
Decker, Nelson
 CA:267
 JA:47
 MA:313, 323, 336, 353

Defries, John D. JA:113

Delafield, John JA:168

Delphi Insurance Co. JA:182

Demson, Ezra JA:194

Denham, John naturalization MA:379

Denmark MA:244

Deyea, E. CA:323

Diggins, John
    CA:210, 211
    JA:22
    MA:168, 196
Diggins, John Jr.
    CA:155
    MA:50
Diggins, John Jr.? CA:153
Diggins, Joseph JA:92
Diggins, Wesley JA:116

Dimick, Elisha CA:582

Dinwiddie & Burnside JA:51
Dinwiddie, D. CA:253, 453

Dinwiddie, David
CA:49, 61, 63-68, 70-86, 88-112, 145, 146, 148-141, 153-157, 159-166, 168, 169, 171-173, 175, 176, 178, 179, 217, 219, 225, 229, 231, 241, 249, 250, 252, 287, 414, 428, 430, 432, 460, 462-464
JA:36, 37, 51, 53, 61, 74, 76, 90,102, 110, 112, 118, 154, 175
MA:24, 44, 50, 54, 100, 205, 240, 253, 275, 290, 293, 295, 299, 301, 346, 396, 438, 503-505, 515
Dinwiddie, David bail
CA:364
MA:450
Dinwiddie, David bailiff MA:13, 23, 25, 48, 175, 242
Dinwiddie, Jno. CA:433
Dinwiddie, William
CA:85, 86, 241, 358, 416
JA:18, 46, 51, 63, 73
MA:144, 206(2), 226, 242, 254, 295, 310, 323, 345, 448, 498
Dinwiddie, William bail CA:250, 254
Dinwiddie, William bail sig MA:300, 301

Disbrow, Henry V. or H. V. JA:155

Dodd, Saml. bail JA:2
Dodd, Samuel F. MA:322
Dodd, Samuel F. bail MA:18

Dodds, Samuel F. bail CA:9

Dodds, Samuel F.
 CA:13, 49, 177, 182, 183, 184, 186, 187, 221, 222, 224, 226, 228, 234, 332
  JA:47, 91
  MA:12, 27, 42, 44, 166, 172, 348

Dodge, Edward MA:161
Dodge, Samuel F. MA:175

Dodrill, John CA:492, 493

Dodsille, John MA:437

Dolton, George MA:516

Donahoo, Wm. sig JA:169

Donaldson, Christopher
  CA:197, 198
  JA:30
  MA:118
Donaldson, Christopher et al. MA:192, 221
Donaldson, Thomas
  CA:197, 198
  MA:118
Donaldson, William
  CA:197, 198
  MA:118

Donge, Edward CA:143

Doremus Suydam & Nixon JA:135, 150

Dorsey, Eli/Ely
CA:113, 115, 116
JA:15
MA:32, 72, 80, 125, 127, 128, 172

Doty, John H.
CA:393
MA:442
Doty, John I./J.
CA:410, 421
MA:382, 455, 461, 485, 502

Douge, Edward JA:22

Douty, John J. CA:335
Douty, John L. MA:437

Dowland, Silas CA:180

Downes, Joshua
CA:558, 563
MA:383

Downs, George H.
CA:6, 7
JA:1
MA:17, 19
Downs, Joshua CA:461, 464, 467, 529, 541, 583

Draper, John   JA:28
   MA:206(2)

Dresden?, Saml. bail JA:199

Droliner, Barzella CA:131
Droliner, Gabriel JA:126
See also Druliner, Drulinger

Druliner, Gabriel JA:90
Druliner, Joseph MA:126
See also Droliner, Drulinger

Drulinger, Daniel
   JA:44
   MA:338
See also Droliner, Druliner

Drum, Jacob
   CA:335, 393, 405, 410, 421, 430
   MA:442, 455, 461, 480, 485, 402, 503, 515
Drum, Jacob sig bail MA:454
Drum, Zachariah JA:111

Drummond, James
   CA:414, 460, 462, 463
   MA:382, 396

Drunvin? Jacob MA:382

Drusse?, Jacob MA:437
Druyer, Simon MA:166

Duffie, John & c. MA:288

Duffy, John
  CA:492
  MA:72, 113, 192, 238, 437

Dugan, James P.
  CA:118, 120-122
  MA:109

Duncan, Samuel C.
  CA:6, 7
  JA:1
  MA:17

Dunham, Ira MA:166
Dunham, Joseph MA:462

Dunn, Jacob bail CA:372

Durkee, Jirch JA:133

Dutton, George JA:86

Dutton, William
   CA: 126, 128   JA:13
   MA:115

Dyer & Freeman
   CA:411
   JA:72
   MA:486
Dyer, Edward MA:439
Dyer, Edward sig MA:161
Dyer, Edwin [crossed out] JA:64
Dyer, Edwin
   CA:349, 368, 411
   JA:61
   MA:161, 312, 393, 439, 452
Dyer, Elwin JA:61

E

Eahart, William
   CA:232, 326, 327, 458, 459, 465
   MA:12, 13, 166, 255
See also Eohart

Earl, George M.
   JA:9
   MA:82

Earley, Jacob MA:383

Early, E. J. JA:144

Early, J. JA:144, 180

Eaton, A. CA:192, 193
Eaton, Daniel C. JA:151

Edwards, J. L. commissioner of pensions MA:123

Egan, William bail
  CA:42, 48
  MA:67
See also Egans, Eggans

Egans, William MA:326, 351, 356
Egans, William bail sig MA:75
Egans, William deceased MA:427
See also Egan, Eggans

Egbert, Asa JA:103, 116, 139
Egbert, Asa sig JA:115
Egbert, Charles MA:12
Egbert, Elisha MA:205, 253
Egbert, John
  CA:240
  JA:108
  MA:238, 279
See also Egburt

Egburt, Charles MA:166
See also Egbert

Eggans, William CA:48
See also Egan, Egans

Eldridge, William M. JP MA:170

Eli, John MA:126

Elkhart County MA:400

Elliott, Hugh
  CA:575-577
  JA:81, 91

Elston, William M. JA:128

England MA:522, 523

Enos, A. W. CA:360, 521
Enos, Alanson W.
  JA:114, 137
  MA:420

Eohart, William CA:329, 331, 334, 336, 338, 340, 342
See also Eahart

Erving, Sample, and others CA:295

Este, David K. MA:244

Evans, Benjamin
  CA:417
  MA:498
Evans, David
  CA:24, 49, 464
  MA:44, 50, 99, 174
Evans, David associate judge [CA:0 – apparently a misplaced page from April 1835]
Evans, David associate judge
  CA:60
  MA:100, 175, 255
Evans, David, associate judge La Porte circuit CA:217
Evans, David judge MA:162

Evens, Calvin R. JA:170

Everhart, Conrad JA:180
Everhart, Conrad bail JA:142

Evert & Osborn JA:180

Everts & Liston CA:540
Everts & McClure CA:549
Everts, G. A.
  CA:430, 434, 435, 577, 579, 590
  JA:159, 199
Everts, G. A. bail JA:200
Everts, G. A. president judge CA:1
Everts, G. A. sig JA:109, 120, 128(2)

Everts, Gustavus   CA:508, 511
   MA:386, 419
Everts, Gustavus A.
   CA:85, 86, 457
   MA:417, 509
Everts, Gustavus A. judge MA:25, 53, 100, 175, 255
Everts, Gustavus A. president judge [CA:0], CA:60
Everts, Gustavus A., president judge 8th Circuit CA: 217
Everts Timothy MA:242
Everts, Timothy C.
   JA:106
   MA:279
Everts, Timothy C. bail JA:152

Evertt, G. A. judge MA:1
Evertt, G.A. judge sig MA:5
Evertt, Gustavus judge MA:1
Evertt, Gustavus A. judge MA:13

Ewing & Sample CA:561, 562
Ewing, Charles W.
   CA:85, 86
   MA:69, 343
Ewing, George W. MA:328, 383, 443
Ewing, William G. MA:328, 383, 443

Examiners of School Teachers MA:97

Fail, Philip
    CA:13, 15, 42, 49, 174, 181, 182, 184, 192, 240
    MA:4, 12, 24, 27, 34, 38, 40, 44, 166, 205, 208, 213, 220, 228, 229, 232, 289
Fail, Phillip bailiff MA:14

Farnsworth, Reuben JA:145
Farnsworth, Stephen JA:145

Farnum, Edward J. JA:143

Fayette County MA:93(2), 121

Ferguson, Jonathan
   CA:140, 142
   JA:8, 22
   MA:159, 160, 173
Ferguson, Wm. CA:24
Ferguson, William bail sig MA:513
See also Furguson

Ferquer, Wm bail JA:76

Ferris, Joel [crossed out] JA:85
Ferris, Joel
   CA:378, 379, 524, 525
   JA:55, 66, 183
   MA:390, 393, 394, 459, 460

Field, G. T.? JA:181
Field, Thomas J.
   CA:132, 521, 522
   JA:87, 145, 165, 199
Field, Thomas J. or T. J. sig JA:180

Fifield, Edward JA:135

Finlay, John CA:558

Finley, David JA:121, 125, 159

Finley, Homer S.
  CA:372, 373
  JA:125
  MA:456, 457
Finley, John
  CA:461, 467, 541, 563, 568, 583
  MA:383
Finley, Samuel
  CA:46
  JA:163

Finly, J. JA:54
Finly, John CA:464

Finn, Enos
  CA:174, 181, 182
  MA:166, 213, 220, 228

Finney, Alanson
  JA:42
  MA:325

Fisher, Henry C.
  CA:201
  JA:30
  MA:223

Fisk, Caleb JA:110, 165

Fisk, Caleb S.
　JA:127, 128
　MA:166
Fisk, Lemuel JA:110, 165

Fitch MA:417
Fitch, Aaron bail sig MA:486
Fitch, Aaron M. bail CA:410
Fitch, F.
　CA:547, 548
　JA:98
Fitch, Fredc. [crossed out] MA:457
Fitch, Frederick
　CA:419, 546, 550, 551
　JA:74
　MA:500
Fitch, Lemuel
　CA:470, 471
　JA:82
　MA:402

Fleming, Daniel F. JA:107

Flemming, Jacob MA:202

Fletcher, Calvin CA:42
Fletcher, John A.
　CA:139, 177, 182-184, 186, 187, 209, 221, 222, 224, 226, 228, 234, 277, 323, 332, 409
　　JA:100, 188
　　MA:95, 166, 175, 366, 526

Fletcher, Peter JA:97
Fletcher, Stoughton JA:120, 158

Flint JA:137
Flint, Electa, Samuel's wife MA:206, 214, 224, 230, 232
Flint, Electa, Samuel's wife deceased MA:290, 291
Flint, Samuel & wife
  JA:27
  MA:205(2)
Flint, Samuel
  CA:108, 185, 203, 225, 227, 230
  MA:167, 206, 214, 224, 229, 230, 232, 275, 279, 284, 290, 291, 322
Flint, Samuel JP CA:194

Forbes, James
  CA:414
  JA:73
  MA:492, 493
Forbes, Thomas
  CA:447
  MA:326, 373, 374, 473, 514

Forby, Homer S. JA:65

Forester, James
  JA:30, 144
  MA:117

Fosdick, George CA:141 page attached
Fosdick, Timothy MA:12

Fosdick, William MA:382

Foster, Andrew
  CA:141 page attached
  JA:181
Foster, Clinton associate judge MA:175, 255, 396
Foster, Clinton
  CA:68, 70-86, 88-112, 145, 146, 148-151, 153-157, 159-166, 168, 169, 171, 172, 175, 176, 178, 179, 217, 219, 229, 231
  JA:28
  MA:100, 174, 206(2)
Foster, Clinton, associate judge La Porte circuit CA: 217
Foster, John D. CA:192
Foster, John J.
  CA:43, 174, 181, 182, 184, 517, 518
  JA:7, 83
  MA:50, 68, 166, 205, 208, 213, 220, 228, 232
Foster, Seneca
  CA:46, 49, 54, 322
  JA:115
  MA:50, 52, 63, 73, 78, 80, 84, 90, 355
Foster, Thomas J.
  JA:45
  MA:166, 226, 322, 341

Frame, Jeremiah MA:167

Francis, Charles CA:203

Francis, Thompson
   CA:132, 338, 339, 341-343   JA:38, 70, 93, 109, 128
   (2), 133, 146, 156, 159, 198
   MA:307, 404, 477, 478
Francis, Willis
   JA:109
   MA:29, 35, 73

Fraser, James MA:166

Fravel, Abraham
   CA:141 page attached
   JA:161
   MA:480
Fravel, John JA:96

Frederickson, Henry
   JA:49, 175
   MA:311, 356, 362, 429
Frederickson, Henry sig JA:115, 196

Freeman, D. B. CA:257
Freeman, David B.
   CA:256, 368, 411
   JA:40, 64, 72, 107, 118, 129, 176
   MA:311, 452
Freeman, Frederick H. CA:257, 258
Freeman, L. B. CA:323

Frost, Gideon JA:139

Fry, William
  CA:529, 558, 568, 583
  MA:383

Frye, Daniel bail JA:113
Frye, William CA:324, 461, 462, 464

Fulsome, Joseph
  CA:144, 232, 326, 327, 329, 331, 334, 336, 338, 340, 342, 458, 459, 465
  MA:161, 167, 255

Fulsum, Joseph CA:323

Furgison, Jonathan sig JA:22 [attached note]

Furguson, Jonathan MA:79
Furguson, William bail sig CA:427
See also Ferguson

Furry, Joseph JA:163

Fursi/Finsi?, Enos MA:208

G

Gale, Thomas W. CA:240

Gallifers, John JA:121

Ganard, John MA:205

Gardner, John MA:3

Garland, Silas CA:63

Garner, James W. MA:488
Garner, Jno. JA:2

Garner, John
  CA:8, 9, 113-116, 133, 174, 197, 198, 212-215
  JA:15, 30
  MA:6, 12, 13, 18, 22, 32, 71, 72, 79, 80, 111, 113, 118, 125, 127, 128, 130, 133, 172, 192, 221, 222
Garner, Thomas J. MA:378
Garner, William G.
  JA:81
  MA:473

Garnet, James JA:127

Garnsey, David E. JA:138

Garrand, John MA:4
Garrand, William MA:4

Garrar, John MA:168

Garrard, John CA:46, 49, 54, 181, 184, 192, 406
Garrard, John MA:12, 50, 63, 73, 80, 84, 90, 166, 208, 213, 220, 229, 232, 481
Garrard, John bail
  CA:34
  MA:57

Garret, Cyrus
  CA:573
  JA:97

Garrison, Henry
  CA:580-582
  JA:100
Garrison, Jane wife of Henry CA:580, 581
Garrison, Lewis CA:582
Garrison, Orestes [crossed out] JA:92
Garrison, Orestes JA:128, 185
Garrison, Orestes bail CA:555

Garvin/Garner, John bail JA:6

Garwood, John
  CA:182, 184, 239
  JA:36
  MA:4, 158, 228, 238, 289, 349
Garwood, Mary MA:334, 368
Garwood, William
  CA:15, 49
  MA:12, 28, 38, 40, 44, 334, 368

Gassehart, Jacob MA:446

Gelbrath, Benjamin Junior bail JA:115
See also Gilbreath

George W. Allen and Company CA:533

Germany MA:244

Gervin, Charles A. and eleven others MA:507

Gewell, Daniel B. bail JA:115

Gibson, J. constable CA:267, 323
Gibson, James
    CA:327, 328, 335-337, 462
    JA:40, 56, 57, 91, 95
    MA:269, 317, 378, 409, 414, 435, 482
Gibson, James bail CA:477
Gibson, James bailiff MA:288
Gibson, James W. JA:128(2)
Gibson, James W. bailiff CA:467

Gilbert, Ezra
    JA:8
    MA:79
Gilbert, Moses JA:163

Gilbreath, Benjamin JA:140
See also Gelbrath

Gillers, James JA:119

Gillespie, Harriet
    CA:570
    JA:84
Gillespie, Harriet admr JA:94
Gillespie, Hugh deceased CA:498, 499

Gilmore, John JA:113

Girton, James I. MA:518

Glosser, Daniel MA:167

Godfroy, Peter sig JA:155

Goff, B. JA:143
Goff, Bernard CA:327
Goff, Brainard
   CA:232, 326, 329, 331, 334, 336, 338, 340, 342, 458, 459, 465
   JA:128(2)
   MA:12, 167, 255

Goldsmith, Ebenetus bail sig MA:347
Goldsmith, Ebinetus bail CA:261

Goode, F. C. ? JA:85

Goodell, Richard H. MA:504
Goodell, Richard H. O. JA:75

Goodwin, I. CA:546
Goodwin, Jonathan CA:546

Gordon, James
   CA:185
   MA:229
Gordon, Lewis MA:32

Gosset, William MA:167
Gosset, William bail
  CA:43
  MA:68

Gould, Ingraham
  CA:254, 255
  JA:38, 140, 159
  MA:166, 303
Gould, Oren
  CA:254, 255
  MA:303
Gould, Orrin JA:38
Gould, Zibena bail JA:93

Gragg, Worlin CA:69, 71, 75, 80, 81, 93-95
See also Gregg, Grigg

Graham, Hugh
  CA:161-165, 171, 217, 219, 229, 231
  JA:189
  MA:50
See also Grayham

Granness, Charles B.
  JA:42
  MA:124, 322
Granness Charles B. & Co. CA:132

Grannis Charles B. MA:236

Granniss Charles [crossed out] MA:233
Granniss, Charles B. MA:309(2), 339
Granniss, Charles B. et al. MA:488

Grant, James JA:145

Grayham, Hugh
 CA:68, 70-86, 88-112, 145, 146, 148-151, 153-157, 159, 160, 166, 168, 169, 172, 175, 176, 178, 179
 MA:100
See also Graham

Great Britain
 CA:456
 MA:9, 11, 24, 70, 304, 379, 389, 509, 510, 522, 523

Green, C. H.
 CA:55
 MA:2
Green, James W. MA:419
Green, John JA:138

Greenfield CA:6, 42

Gregg, P. S. CA:286
Gregg, Worlen/Worlin
 CA:102
 MA:189, 264, 399
See also Gragg, Grigg

Gregory, Niles JA:97
Gregory, Niles bail JA:107

Griesell, John
　JA:72
　MA:391
See also Grisell, Grissell

Griffin, Daniel
　CA:232, 326-329, 331, 334, 336, 338, 340, 342, 465
　MA:167, 255
Griffin, David CA:458, 459
Griffin, Samuel
　CA:68, 70-86, 88-112, 145, 146, 148-151, 153-157, 159-166, 168, 169, 171, 172, 175, 176, 178, 179, 217, 219, 229, 231
　MA:50, 100
Griffin, Tolcott
　CA:464
　MA:382

Griffith, Harriet MA:372
Griffith, Hiram MA:372
Griffith, Nehemiah deceased MA:372, 487
Griffith, Nehemiah heirs MA:487
Griffith, Sarah MA:372

Grigg & Elliott CA:575-577

Grigg, John
    CA:575-577
    JA:81, 91
Grigg, Worlin CA:96, 100
See also Gragg, Gregg

Grisell/Grissell, John
    JA:190
    MA:484, 485
See also Griesell

Griswold, Chester JA:133

Grover & Williams
    CA:531
    JA:101
Grover, Isaiah MA:298
Grover, J. CA:323
Grover, Jeremiah
    CA:324, 334, 365-368, 383, 384, 412, 413, 417, 418, 531, 575-577
    JA:64, 69, 73, 81, 86, 91, 94, 96, 103, 115, 119
    MA:298, 343, 436, 450, 451, 470, 471, 499
Grover, Josiah
    CA:365-368, 383, 384, 412, 413, 417, 418, 575
    JA:64, 69, 73, 81, 91
    MA:343, 450, 451, 470, 471, 499

H

H & T. Wheeler
  CA:235, 236, 241, 242, 249, 252, 253, 343, 344, 361-363, 371, 497
    JA:26, 27, 51, 53
    MA:89, 194, 254, 294, 416, 453
H. & V. Wheeler JA:35

Haas, J. CA:346
Haas, Jacob [crossed out] MA:207

Haas, Jacob
 CA:298, 300, 301, 317, 321, 345, 381, 382, 409, 417, 511, 524
 JA:37, 44, 59, 68, 75, 85, 113, 123, 154, 177
 MA:215, 216, 218, 225, 291, 292, 335, 340, 342, 352, 359, 360, 426, 469, 498, 506
Haas, Jacob sig JA:88
Haas, Jacob D. MA:485
See also Hass

Hacker, Jonathan CA:421
Hacker, Jonathan M.
 CA:406, 409
 JA:51
 MA:251, 294, 481, 485, 502

Hackley JA:125
Hackley, J. H sig? MA:520
Hackley, Joseph H.
 CA:360
 JA:63, 110, 156, 183, 191, 200
 MA:448, 519

Hagenbuch, William [inserted paper] JA:126
Hagenbuch, Wm. bail JA:140

Hagenbuck, William JA:143, 171

Hagenbush Wm JA:113

Hahn, Christian W.
  CA:412, 413   JA:69
  MA:470

Haight, Augustus JA:117
Haight, Henry JA:179
Haight, Nathaniel JA:117
Haight, Richard JA:179

Hains/Haines, Nathan MA:12, 25

Hales, Jacob MA:309(2)

Hall, A. A. JA:29
Hall, Abraham A.
  CA:161, 222, 223, 477, 478
  JA:24, 32, 78, 109
  MA:184, 211, 218-220, 231, 232, 239, 268, 269, 409, 410, 430, 431
Hall, Abram CA:180
Hall, Abram A.
  CA:184, 185, 221
  JA:152
Hall, Daniel
  CA:193
  MA:193
Hall, George B. judge in Ohio CA:488, 490
Hall, Israel CA:180

Hall, Jacob R.   CA:335, 337, 393, 405, 410, 415, 421, 427, 430
    MA:382, 436, 437, 442, 455, 461, 480, 485, 492, 502, 503, 512, 515
Hall, James JA:160
Hall, John P. JA:118
Hall, S. D. CA:142
Hall, Samuel D.
    CA:140
    MA:159, 173
Hall, Susan P. admx JA:93
Hall, Wesley sig JA:148

Halland, Henry MA:196

Hallet, Melinda JA:129

Halstead/Halsted, Samuel
    CA:134-137, 263, 264
    JA:15, 36
    MA:117, 122, 126, 130-132, 162, 234, 288, 437
Halstead, Samuel sig MA:134
See Holstead

Hamell & Henning JA:168

Hamilton County, Ohio
    CA:213, 215
    MA:243, 244

Hamilton, John CA:513 JA:27
  MA:167, 191, 200
Hamilton, John sig JA:84

Hann, Geo. W. JA:156

Hanna, Andrew CA:321

Hannah & Merryfield CA:212
Hannah, W. C.
  CA:384, 413
  JA:66, 99
Hannah, W. C. JP CA:573
Hannah, W. C. sig JA:141
Hannah, William C.
  CA:397, 402, 448-451
  JA:108, 144
  MA:96, 374, 376, 495-497
Hannah, William C. bail
  CA:92, 144
  MA:147
Hannah, William C. commissioner MA:494
Hannah, William C. JP
  CA:530-532, 574
  MA:521
Hannah, Wm. C. bail sig MA:161

Hannegan & Hannah JA:141, 173, 181

Hannuman, Jacob MA:173

Happ, Abram bail CA:408
Happ, Jacob JA:66

Harman, David
  CA:61, 62, 64-67, 141 page attached, 173
  MA:50, 54
Harman, David bail JA:85

Harmeson/Harmison, Samuel Senr.
  CA:160
  MA:12, 25

Harmon, A. CA:286
Harmon, David
  JA:149
  MA:28

Harn/Ham, John JA:179

Harper, Abraham R. JA:150
Harper, John JA:150

Harris, John
  CA:185, 479, 480
  JA:82
  MA:229

Harris, Richard
  CA:15, 48   MA:12, 34, 38, 40, 42, 95Harris, Richard bail
  CA:12, 13
  MA:30
Harris, Timothy JA:149
Harris, William
  CA:23, 24
  JA:4
  MA:47

Harrison, A & A. W. JA:14
Harrison, A. MA:389
Harrison, A. W.
  CA:46, 323, 527
  JA:75, 136
  MA:50, 389
Harrison, Abraham
  CA:260
  MA:227
Harrison, Abraham W.
  CA:188
  MA:118, 131, 166, 232
Harrison, Abram CA:260
Harrison, Abram V. CA:192

Harrison, Abram W.
   CA:189, 517, 525, 526
   JA:112, 128(2), 153, 154, 157, 172, 188
   MA:305, 347, 478, 484
   Harrison, Abram W. or A. W. sig JA:83Harrison, Alfred
   CA:188, 189, 192, 260
   JA:112, 136, 157
   MA:118, 131, 227, 232, 347, 478, 484
   Harrison, Elizabeth JA:202
   Harrison, Francis P. CA:131
   Harrison, Richard bail JA:2
   Harrison, Samuel JA:75
   Harrison, Wm. H. MA:244

Harrison/Hamison?/Humison?, Samuel MA:506

Hart, Ralph S. MA:417

Hartman, William MA:120, 239, 335

Hartshorn, John
   CA:35
   MA:61, 102
   Hartshorn, William [crossed out] JA:111
   Hartshorn, William [inserted page] JA:138
   Hartshorn, William JA:119, 138, 145, 167, 170, 173, 178, 179, 182, 183, 186, 198

Harvey, John MA:166

Harvey, Jonathan S. CA:417
MA:498

Hass, Jacob JA:129, 176
MA:50, 166
See also Haas

Hatch, Arvet M. JA:107

Hatfield, E. J. MA:480
Hatfield, E. S. CA:404
Hatfield, Edward J.
JA:48, 71
MA:278, 358
Hatfield, James CA:194
Hatfield, M. C.
CA:193, 194, 548
JA:48
MA:480
Hatfield, M. C. bail
CA:267
JA:34
Hatfield, Moses [crossed out] O. MA:41
Hatfield, Moses MA:49 1/2, 464, 465, 481

Hatfield, Moses C.
  CA:108-110, 144, 259, 267, 322, 404, 406, 550
  JA:4, 21, 32, 45, 49, 67, 71, 95   MA:35, 49, 120,
  124, 155, 156, 161, 234, 239, 340, 355, 363, 370, 421,
  422, 480, 482
Hatfield, Moses C. bail
  CA:227, 235, 268
  MA:281, 336, 358, 369
Hatfield, Richard JA:128

Hathaway & Chapman
  CA:131
  JA:112, 127, 141

Hawill, William B. MA:223

Hawking, William clerk MA:100

Hawkins, William [crossed out] MA:102
Hawkins, William
  CA:243, 448, 449
  MA:14, 25, 99, 108, 134, 174, 495
Hawkins, William clerk MA:98, 175, 255, 396
Hawkins, Wm. court clerk
  CA:61
  MA:80

Hazleton, John MA:372

Heald, Arba
CA:13, 15, 230, 265, 277, 281, 287, 313, 314-316, 467
JA:49 MA:12, 27, 38, 167, 316, 322, 324, 346, 351, 354, 359, 361, 365-367, 507Heald, Arba sig JA:48
See also Heuld

Hefner, John MA:351
Hefner, John admr JA:94

Hemanway, Henry C. sig JA:170

Henderson, Charles N. JA:100, 150
Henderson, Richard JP MA:169, 170

Hendricks/Henrix, Enos
   JA:25
   MA:158, 193

Henry, Charles CA:327
Henry, Charles W.
   CA:326
   JA:57
   MA:166, 191, 414
Henry, Thomas sig JA:202
Henry, William JA:202

Henton, Peter MA:103, 104

Herr, Henry V. JA:12Herr, John bail CA:132

Hesston/Henton?, Peter CA:62

Heuld, Arba MA:284
See also Heald

Heus, Richard B. MA:334

Hewes, Richard B. MA:378

Hews, John F. CA:192
Hews, R. B.
  JA:50, 152
  MA:370
Hews, Richard B. [MA:527]
Hews, Richard B.
  CA:111, 112, 232, 233, 310-312, 331, 421, 454, 455
  JA:21, 56
  MA:156, 157, 242, 321, 368, 373, 377, 413, 463, 502, 513
Hews, Richard B. bail CA:258
Hews, Richard B. bail sig MA:312
Hews, Richard B. sig JA:76, 180
Hews, Richard D. MA:331
See also Hughs

Hibbard & Co. JA:108

Hickman/Hickmann, Jacob V. CA:232, 326, 327, 331, 336, 340, 342, 458, 459, 465
 MA:167, 255
Hickman, Jacob Y. CA:329, 334, 338

Higgins, William
 CA:265
 JA:21, 50
 MA:159, 377

Highley/Highly, James MA:2, 12, 166, 191

Hill, David MA:166
Hill, Edward MA:166

Hills, John L. CA:141 page attached

Hinton, Peter
 JA:200
 MA:50

Hiorth, H. C. CA:53
Hiorth, Hans A. CA:52
See Horth

Hitchcock, James JA:136, 138
Hitchcock, John JA:136, 138
Hitchcock, Peter judge in Ohio CA:486

Hixon, Ashton D. JA:32

Hixon, J. Jun. ? CA:192
Hixon, Jeremiah
  CA:188
  MA:131, 232
Hixon, Jeremy
  CA:190-192
  JA:38, 130, 186
Hixon, Jeremy Jr. MA:306
Hixon/Nixon, James bail MA:16

Hixson, Quincy MA:227

Hobart, Joshua
  CA:318, 320
  JA:47, 163
  MA:335, 349

Hobart, Joshua bail JA:154

Hobbs, Joshua T.
  CA:19, 129
  JA:14
  MA:117

Hobert, Joshua bail JA:100

Hobson, Evan B. JA:97

Hodges, George C. JA:117

Hodges, Hiram H.   JA:117   MA:526
Hodges, Hiram N. JA:106

Hoffman, Charles
  CA:522
  JA:89

Hogal, John H. MA:78
Hogal, John L. JA:9
Hogal, John S. MA:89

Hoge, Thomas S.
  CA:210, 211
  JA:22
  MA:50, 168

Hogue, Thomas J. MA:196
Hogue, Thomas S. CA:210

Holbrook, Hiram P. bail JA:87

Holeston, Horace G. MA:435

Holland, Henry
  CA:209
  JA:29
  MA:197, 212, 221

Hollaway, Stephen CA:405
  MA:480

Holliday, John
  CA:498
  JA:99
  Holliday, John naturalization MA:522

Hollister, Horace CA:180
Hollister/Holister, Horace G.
  CA:335-337
  JA:40
  MA:317

Holloway, Stephen MA:12, 25, 166

Holman, David CA:46

Holmes, William
  JA:15, 40
  MA:12, 119, 129, 310
Holmes, William Jr.
  JA:11
  MA:106

Holstead/Holsted, Samuel
  CA:556, 557, 559
  JA:82
  See Halstead

Holt, David A. CA:46, 49, 54
MA:50, 63, 73, 80, 90

Hopkins, George F.
CA:461, 494, 529, 541, 558, 563, 583
Hopkins, George F. bail CA:244
Hopkins, George F. bail sig MA:296
Hopkins, George K. MA:383
Hopkins, John
CA:11, 12
JA:2
MA:26, 27, 30

Horne, J. C. constable CA:285

Hornwall, Thomas CA:277

Horth/Hoith?, Hans E. MA:81
Horth/Hiorth, Hans E. JA:9
See Hiorth

Hough, Ithridge MA:385
Hough, Olmstead
CA:306, 308, 309
MA:294, 344

Howe, J. C. CA:323
Howe, John B.
JA:174
MA:69

Howell & McCarty JA:96
Howell, J. C.
  CA:209, 286, 323, 324
  MA:305
Howell, James
  CA:282
  MA:367
Howell, James C.
  CA:414, 460, 462, 463
  JA:114
  MA:365, 382, 396
Howell, William B.
  CA:201
  JA:30

Hoxie?, J. C. CA:285

Hoyt, L. CA:54
Hoyt, Lucius
  CA:53
  JA:9
  MA:90

Hubbill, Richard H. CA:480, 482

Hubble, Richard H. MA:452

Huchins, James JA:32

Hughs, Arthur JA:119
Hughs/Hughes, Arthur et al.
JA:71
MA:483
Hughs, John MA:25
Hughs,/Hughes John F.
CA:182, 184, 203
JA:31
MA:12, 166, 224, 228, 232
Hughs, John M. JA:119
See also Hews

Hull, Daniel JA:26

Humphrey, Joseph JA:120

Hunt, Horace
JA:86
MA:516
Hunt, John S. MA:253
Hunt, Phineas
CA:406, 415, 461, 462, 467, 558, 565
MA:383, 481, 492, 503
Hunt, Richard [crossed out] JA:122
Hunt, Stephen G. CA:141 page attached
Hunt, Walter P. JA:122
Hunt, William
CA:49, 54, 133

Huntington, Hallam JA:181

Huntsman, Howel/Howell
  CA:232, 326, 327, 329, 331, 334, 336, 338, 340, 342, 458, 459, 465
  MA:167, 255
Huntsman, Howell sig JA:113

Hupp, Abraham JA:96, 165, 194, 202
Hupp, Abraham bail MA:483
Hupp, Abram JA:86
Hupp, Jacob
  CA:376
  MA:459

Hutchens & Saylor JA:101
Hutchens, James
  CA:543, 545, 561, 562
  JA:82
  MA:216, 237, 321, 325
Hutchens, James sig JA:101

Hutchins CA:324
Hutchins, James [crossed out] MA:218
Hutchins, James bail [crossed out] JA:60
Hutchins, James
  CA:1, 2, 48, 182, 183, 186, 225, 323, 543
  JA:1, 8, 29, 42
  MA:7, 12, 13, 43, 80, 196, 212, 322, 447, 455, 483
Hutchins, Samuel CA:532
See also Huchins

IJ

Indianapolis CA:516

Ingoldsby, Felix JA:125

Inhabitants of Congr. Township No. 38 North of R. 3 W. of the 2nd principal meridian MA:214, 291
Inhabitants of T[ownship] 38 MA:225

Inman, Hiram [inserted paper] JA:126
Inman, Hiram
    CA:132, 193, 374, 375, 578, 579
    JA:38, 66, 113, 114, 126, 127, 129, 169, 193, 200
    MA:305, 306, 457, 458

Inwood, Richard JA:87, 93

Iowa JA:113

Ireland MA:163, 252

Irvine, Thomas naturalization sig mark MA:252

Irwin, Arthur MA:12, 13
Irwin, William
  CA:532
  JA:104

Isle of Man CA:456

Ithridge & Hough JA:45
Ithridge/Ithrige, Samuel
  CA:306, 308, 309
  MA:294, 344

Ives, Charles MA:12, 13, 97, 323
Ives, Charles county agent MA:251
Ives, Charles deceased MA:427

IN COURT IN LA PORTE

Janes/Lanes?, Henry F. MA:50
Janes, E. CA:321
Janes, Eli CA:532
Janes, Henry MA:12
Janes, William
   CA:406
   MA:481

Jefferson County, New York CA:55

Jeffries?, George JA:145

Jessup, John
   CA:139, 203, 286, 416   JA:246, 378
Jessup, John bailiff MA:288, 349, 396, 517
Jessup, John constable
   CA:262, 321, 347, 348, 350, 352, 353, 355, 403,
   406, 407, 409, 419-421, 426, 431, 433 530
   MA:164, 244(2), 245, 251, 381, 392

Jewel, Harrison JA:160

Jewell, Daniel B. JA:116

Joel Ferris & Co. CA:378

Johnson, Cornelius MA:214, 291
Johnson, John C. JA:181
Johnson, Nathan CA:61, 63-67, 173
   MA:50, 54
Johnson, Samuel
   CA:147, 148
   JA:23
   MA:177, 211
Johnson, Solon
   CA:131
   JA:185
Johnson, Solon bail JA:87, 89, 116, 179, 182

Jones, Isaac N. MA:251, 323, 427

Jones, J. CA:209

Jones, James F. MA:95
Jones, John   CA:318, 341
  MA:324, 325, 329
  JA:26
Jones, John bail MA:435
Jones, John H.
  JA:51
  MA:178, 253, 294
  JA:42
Jones, Levi D. MA:164, 165, 194
Jones, Myron CA:322, 355
Jones, S. /L.? CA:23
Jones, Stephen JA:171
Jones, Thomas D.
  JA:67
  MA:171, 217, 383, 462
Jones, Thomas D. bail MA:247, 248
Jones, W. D. CA:321
Jones, William D.
  CA:62, 116, 137, 141, 208, 209, 228, 394, 396-398, 401, 402, 406, 425, 426, 557
  JA:33, 34, 43, 69, 76
  MA:50, 103, 122, 128, 129, 132, 159, 171, 206, 206 (2), 217, 225, 235, 236, 239, 240, 281, 305, 309(2), 332, 366, 442, 474, 475, 481, 512
Jones, William D. bail MA:247, 248
Jones, William J. CA:277

Jordan, Joshua sig JA:170

Judson, Lewis B. CA:18
 MA:37
 JA:3, 5

Jurnegan & Bradley/Bradly CA:534, 535, 539, 540
Jurnegan, Joseph MA:417, 420
Jurnegan, Joseph prosecutor MA:397
See also Jernegan

Justice, William
 CA:13, 15, 17, 177, 182-184, 186, 187, 221, 222, 224, 226, 228, 234, 332
 MA:12, 27, 38, 40, 42, 44, 166, 175

K

Kankakee Township CA:47

Kankee [Kankakee?] CA:572

Keath/Heath? Adam MA:511

Keely, William JA:90

Keer, Joseph MA:90

Keeth, Lewis MA:42
Keeth, Lewis bail MA:46

Keith, Adam
  CA:49, 62, 116, 137, 141, 144, 247
  JA:53, 67
  MA:12, 44, 50, 103, 128, 132, 159, 161, 299, 461
Keith, Lewis
  CA:13
  MA:12, 27, 34
Keith, Lewis bail CA:17
Keith, Lewis bail sig mark
  CA:322
  MA:355
  JA:102
Keith, Michael MA:316, 351, 361

Kellogg, Ashley R. JA:97, 181
Kellogg, Charles JA:151

Kellough, David JA:6

Kendall, Samuel CA:178

Kendle, Samuel CA:323

Kennedy, Edward MA:386

Kerr, J. & S. CA:54
Kerr, Joseph
  CA:18, 53, 62, 141, 144, 240
  JA:2, 3, 5, 9
  MA:20, 37, 50, 103, 132, 159, 161, 289

Kerr, Joseph bail [crossed out] JA:8
Kerr, Joseph bail
  CA:30, 32, 33, 41
  JA:6
Kerr, Joseph bail sig MA:55, 65, 76
Kerr, Samuel
  CA:53
  JA:9
  MA:90

Kerry, John L. [crossed out] JA:7

Kewley, John JA:151

Kieth, Michael JA:49

Kilgore, Jesse JA:163

Killough, David, Monroe County library treasurer MA:168

Kimball, Moses JA:107

Kimberly, George CA:131

King, John
  CA:122-124
  MA:72, 113

King, Victor
   CA:122-124   MA:72, 113

Kinney Simon JA:171

Knapp, John
   CA:451, 452, 475, 476
   JA:79
   MA:4, 5, 14, 196, 371, 432
See also Knopp

Knickerbacker, James [MA:527]

Knight, George C. JA:128, 169, 185

Knopp, John MA:15
See also Knapp

Koontz, John JA:123

L

Lacy, J. S. CA:47, 54
Lacy, John S.
  CA:42
  MA:14, 103

Lafayette
  CA:52, 53
  MA:507

Lagrange Circuit Court JA:5
Lagrange County CA:18, 19

Laird, John MA:356
Laird, Joseph
  JA:67, 94
  MA:326, 351, 356, 427, 463
Laird, Peter MA:356

Lake, Harry
  JA:70
  MA:404, 405, 477

Lamb, Pliny
  CA:310-312
  JA:50, 61, 62
  MA:312, 321, 331, 373, 393, 439

Lamson, Silas [crossed out] JA:117
Lamson, Silas
  CA:522, 523, 569
  JA:88, 89, 135, 144, 152

Landis, Jacob
  CA:116
  MA:107
Landis, Philip
  CA:116
  MA:107

Landon, Nelson
  CA:46, 48, 131
  MA:12, 25, 52, 75, 80, 121

Lane, Ebenezer judge in Ohio CA:486

Lang, Stanbery/Stanbury/Stansberry/Stansbury
CA:278
JA:49
MA:322, 365

Langdon, John [crossed out] JA:8
Langdon, John
CA:29-32, 41, 129, 130
JA:6, 7, 14
MA:50, 55, 64, 76, 117, 118
Langdon, N. JA:14

Laporte Land Office CA:538

Lary, Daniel
CA:196, 197
MA:116, 120, 215

Laughlin, James
CA:62, 116, 372, 373, 557
MA:50, 103, 122, 128, 129, 131, 456
JA:65

Lawson/Lauson, James
CA:332, 333
JA:37, 55, 63, 90
MA:214, 249, 270, 292, 391, 410, 430, 445, 516

Layman, Joseph MA:382
Layman, Joshua
 CA:414, 460, 462, 463
 MA:396

Leach, Abiel Q. D.
 CA:254, 255, 505
 JA:38, 51, 88
 MA:250, 294, 303

Leaming, Daniel M.
 CA:182, 187
 JA:104
Leaming, Judah [crossed out] MA:102
Leaming, Judah
 CA:254, 255
 JA:38, 157
 MA:99, 108, 303
Leaming, Judah associate judge
 CA:1, 60
 MA:25, 53, 100
Leaming, Judah bail CA:22
Leaming, Judah judge MA:1, 11, 162
See also Leming, McLeaming

Lee, Ebenezer Y.
 CA:463, 495, 496
 JA:78, 79, 128(2)
 MA:444-445, 461

Leeds, Joseph JA:193

Leek, John
   CA:580-582
   JA:100

Leming, Judah associate judge
   [CA:0 – misplaced page from April 1835]
   MA:13
See also Leaming, McLeaming

Lemon, John M. [crossed out] MA:491
Lemon, John M.
   CA:394, 428, 430
   JA:76, 90, 143, 155
   MA:50, 382, 594, 515
Lemon, John M., Major CA:395, 400
Lemon, Samuel JA:164

Leonard, Silas
   CA:130
   JA:14
   MA:118

Lewis, John MA:106
Lewis, John bail CA:173
Lewis, Orrin
   CA:185
   MA:229

Lewis, William G. judge in Ohio CA:488, 490

Leyre?, Edwin/Ewin/Edward/Ewald? MA:525

Lies/Lag/Lacy, John S. CA:41

Likins, Joseph W. CA:287
Likins, Joseph bail CA:318, 482
See also Lykins

Lilly, Calvin
   CA:12, 14, 17, 20, 23, 24, 115
   JA:1, 4
   MA:16, 25, 26, 32, 34, 36, 47, 48, 59
Lilly, Calvin bail
   CA:21
   MA:21, 33
Lilly, Calvin Jr. CA:5

Lima Township, Lagrange County CA:18

Lindsay, Elijah
   JA:60, 70
   MA:413, 432, 442, 443, 475, 483
Lindsay, Elijah bail MA:227, 230
Lindsay, William
   JA:72
   MA:484
See also Lindsey, Linsey

Lindsey, Elijah
  CA:393, 454, 455
  MA:331, 341, 370
  Lindsey, Elijah bail CA:181
  See also Lindsay, Linsey

Line, Benjamin MA:166
Line, Jonathan
  CA:464
  MA:382

Linsey CA:386, 387
Linsey, Elijah CA:324, 385
See also Lindsay, Lindsey

Liston MA:428
Liston & Bradley CA:290, 294, 295
Liston Merryfield & Hannah CA:489, 491, 582
Liston Niles & Everts CA:535
Liston, J. sig JA:155
Liston, J. A.
  CA:26, 27, 44, 385, 393, 481, 483, 485, 588
  JA:2, 138, 176
Liston, J. A. sig
  JA:107, 136
  MA:353 [paper pasted in]
Liston, J. H. CA:304
Liston, J. H. sig JA:147
Liston, J.R. JA:170
Liston, J. W. JA:9

Liston, Jonathan A.
JA:31
MA:2, 104, 178, 230
Liston, Jonathan A. bail
CA:21, 38, 479, 480, 482, 587
MA:33, 91

Livley, Elijah CA:323

Lockhart, James
CA:4
JA:1
MA:15

Logansport MA:93(2), 158
Logansport Canal Telegraph
CA:207
MA:126, 158
Logansport Telegraph MA:111

Loller, Thomas CA:60

Loney, Jesse JA:141

Long, Elizabeth CA:114
Long, John
CA:335-337, 458, 459
JA:41, 62, 67, 80, 152
MA:317, 369, 408, 409, 417, 418, 420, 421, 445, 465, 466, 468

Long, Robert
  CA:70, 72-74, 97, 98, 180
  MA:190, 265, 399

Loomis, Ralph
  CA:225, 227, 230, 265, 282, 287, 302, 312, 317, 322, 486, 488-490
  JA:102
  MA:102, 167, 275, 279, 284, 293, 322, 335, 346, 351, 354, 355, 359, 365-367, 373
  See also Lornis

Loring, Silas JA:50
Loring, Wright bail CA:279

Lornis, Ralph CA:277
See also Loomis

Loveless & More
  CA:194
  MA:194
Loveless, Joseph R. CA:194, 195

Loving, Ralph MA:437
Loving, Silas
  JA:91
  MA:360, 365
Loving, Silas sig mark [MA:527]
Loving, Wright bail MA:365

Low, D. JA:88, 95, 128, 135-137, 139, 141, 146

Low, Daniel
   CA:511, 513, 515, 583, 585, 586
   JA:93, 110, 145, 163, 166
Low, N. W. JA:88, 95, 128, 135-137, 139, 141, 146
Low, Nathan W.
   CA:511, 513, 515, 583, 585, 586
   JA:93, 110, 145, 163, 166
Low, Peter [crossed out] MA:217
Low, Peter MA:28, 175

Lowe, Jacob B. MA:169Lowe, Peter
   CA:17, 177, 182-184, 186, 187, 221, 222, 224, 226, 228, 234, 332
   MA:4, 12, 42, 44

Lucas, Abbott/Albert? MA:498

Lucas, Albert
   CA:240, 323, 337, 417, 427
   MA:289, 436, 512
Lucas, Daniel MA:12
Lucas, Frances MA:238
Lucas, Francis
   CA:239
   JA:36
   MA:158, 289, 349

Lucy, John S. MA:25, 67

Lumes? [Turner??], Samuel MA:373

Lusk, Henry sig JA:141, 144, 169, 175

Luther, James H.
  JA:53
  MA:320

Lykins, Joseph MA:12, 13, 325, 346
Lykins, Joseph W. bail CA:485
Lykins, Joseph W. sig JA:162
See also Likins

M

M'Broom, Andrew M:29, 30

M'Clure, Arthur MA:2
M'Clure, Arthur JP MA:6
M'Clure, Christopher bailiff MA:2

M'Culloch, Hugh MA:2

M'Givens, Hugh MA:2

M'Kinster, Noble MA:2
See also McKinstry

Madison CA:123, 124, 127, 128

Magher, Peter JA:129

Magie, David JA:181

Maine, John CA:385-392

Makham, Israel CA:462, 464

Mallet, Hiram
  JA:37
  MA:217, 292

Malone, William CA:17
Malone, Wilson/Willson
  CA:13, 133, 177, 182-184, 186, 187, 221, 222, 224, 226, 228, 234, 332
  JA:100
  MA:12, 27, 34, 40, 44, 130, 166, 175

Maltby, Elbridge JA:137

Man, Henry V. MA:114

Mann, Jacob CA:34

Manning & Wick CA:432

Manning, Henry
  CA:432
  JA:61
  MA:438
Manning, Henry & c. MA:293

Mansfield, Thomas W. JA:167

Maple, W. M. CA:589
Maple, William M. bail CA:588

Margeson, Margaret JA:199

Marion County MA:190, 265, 399

Markham, Horace
  CA:13, 15, 17
  JA:38
  MA:12, 27, 34, 38, 40, 44, 224, 252, 303
Markham, Israel/Isreal
  CA:461, 467, 494, 529, 563, 568, 583
  MA:12, 13, 383
Markham, Israel bail
  CA:500
  JA:99

Marrin, Asa M. CA:335

Marsh, Mordecai L. JA:147

Martin, Anderson
  JA:6
  MA:55
Martin, Gale JA:125
Martin, Lyman
  CA:337
  MA:382, 436
Martin, Orin/Orrin
  CA:225, 230, 265, 277, 281, 302, 312, 317, 322, 406, 410, 417
  MA:50, 167, 275, 283, 335, 351, 354, 355, 359, 365-367, 373, 481, 498
Martin, Owen MA:485

Mase, Abner MA:253

Mashon, William H. JA:186

Mason, Alva/Alvah
  CA:228, 244, 394, 399
  JA:29
  MA:217, 297, 302, 382
Mason, Alvah sig JA:52
Mason, Alvah sig? MA:171
Mason, Howard
  CA:414, 460, 462, 463
  MA:382, 396
Mason, Jasper JA:187
Mason, John W. JA:139
Mason, Levi MA:456

Massey, Levi sig JA:114
Massey, Mordecai JA:70
Massey, Mordecai divorce MA:329, 477
Massey, Susannah JA:70
Massey, Susannah divorce MA:329, 477

Mathews/Matthew/Matthews, Clark
   CA:277, 335-337
   JA:41
   MA:318, 435
Mathews, Clark bail sig MA:366
Mathews, John CA:193

Matterson, Schuyler H. CA:131

Maxon, Doct. CA:193, 194
Maxon, Lee H. CA:434
Maxon, Lee H. S.
   JA:55
   MA:338
Maxon, Lee H. T.
   JA:44, 134, 167, 191
   MA:393, 394, 459
Maxon, Lee H. T. bail CA:579

Maxson, Dr. William MA:97
Maxson, Lee H. T. JA:66

Maxton, Lee H. T. JA:76
Maxton, Lee H. G. MA:512

May, Ezra JA:160

Mayhew, E. JA:101
Mayhew, Elisha
  CA:243
  JA:52
  MA:296

Mc??hey, Williams MA:93 (2)

McCafferty, Edward
  CA:78, 79, 87-91, 180, 453
  JA:18, 59
  MA:145, 146, 275, 276, 411, 425
McCafferty, Edward M. [crossed out] MA:148, 431
McCafferty, Edward M.
  CA:86
  MA:147

McCartney, William
  JA:32, 37, 67, 115, 189
  MA:76, 84, 85, 87, 125, 226, 233, 238, 292, 463
McCartney, William M. MA:216

McCarty & Howell JA:114
McCarty, Benjamin
  CA:17, 177, 182-184, 186, 187, 221, 222, 224, 226, 228, 234, 332
  MA:12, 28, 34, 42, 44, 45, 166, 175
McCarty, J. JA:153, 154

McCarty, Nicholas JA:114

McCendry, John bail sig mark [slip pasted in] MA: 289

McClain, Jesse MA:71, 252
McClain, John Jr. MA:169, 386

McClane, Jesse
  CA:15, 184
  MA:79, 112, 224
McClane, Jesse bail
  CA:184
  MA:231
McClane, John CA:154, 159
McClane/McClain, Andrew H. bail sig MA:298
See also McLain, McLane

McClintock/McClintick, Joseph
  CA:461, 464, 495, 529, 541, 558, 568, 583
  MA:383

McClure & Everts CA:550, 551
McClure, A. JP CA:22
McClure, A. M.
  MA:171
McClure, A. M. JP CA:3
McClure, Andrew bail CA:247

McClure, Arthur [crossed out]
  JA:52
  MA:129
McClure, Arthur
  CA:4, 5, 20, 125, 126, 133, 134, 244, 245, 492, 563, 583
  JA:12, 13, 51, 94
  MA:12, 28, 50, 107, 113-115, 130, 171, 192, 238, 288, 295, 386, 437
McClure, Arthur bail
  CA:29, 117, 218, 220
  JA:114
  MA:49
McClure, Arthur bail sig MA:259
McClure, Arthur JP
  CA:1, 2, 21
  MA:9
McClure, Arthur M. MA:297
McClure, C.
  CA:3, 548, 552
  JA:143
McClure, Charles
  CA:46, 49, 54, 428, 430, 496, 501, 502, 504, 547
  JA:46, 113, 143, 186
  MA:50, 63, 73, 80, 84, 90
McClure, Charles sig JA:49, 76, 78, 109, 142, 146
McClure, Christopher
  CA:185, 192, 503, 504
  JA:12, 13 ["Brother Christopher"]
  MA:12, 46, 114, 171, 229, 232

McClure, Christopher bail   CA:24, 495
  JA:4
  MA:48
McClure, Christopher bail sig MA:3
McClure, Christopher bailiff MA:25, 48
McClure, Christopher sig JA:85

McCollom, George MA:320
McCollom, John M. MA:413

McCollum, David
  JA:37
  MA:293
McCollum, George JA:41

McCord, George
  CA:62
  MA:103, 114
McCord, James
  CA:462
  JA:200

McCormic, Alexander
  JA:94
  MA:462

McCormick, John JA:137, 139, 159, 192

McCreary, Amos W.
  CA:519
  JA:89
McCullum, David M. MA:249

McCurdy, John JA:199
McCurdy, John bail sig mark CA:241

McCure, Charles MA:190

McDaniel, Alfred MA:93, 110, 121

McFinley, Samuel
  CA:23, 24
  JA:4
McFinley, Samuel M. MA:47

McFinnan, Daniel judge in Ohio CA:488, 490

McGivan, Hugh CA:3

McGiven & Hale JA:22
McGiven, Hugh
  CA:140, 142
  JA:1, 22, 39, 62, 187
  MA:173, 309, 442
McGiven, Hugh naturalization MA:163
McGiven, Hugh M. MA:159
McGiven, Hugh M. sig MA:160

McGivens, Hugh CA:10
McGrohlin, E. CA:321

McKee, Thomas H.
  CA:414, 460, 462, 463
  MA:382, 396

McKennan, Jonathan
  CA:180
  JA:12

McKinsey, John Gordon MA:116

McKinstrey, R. JA:14

McKinstry, Noble
  CA:13, 49, 131
  MA:12, 27, 34, 40, 44, 121
McKinstry, Rockwell
  CA:131
  MA:121
See also M'Kinster

McLain, Jesse MA:386
McLain, John Jr. CA:303

McLane, Jesse
  CA:203
  JA:38
  MA:12, 303

McLane, John Jr. CA:303, 305
   JA:44
   MA:305, 336
   See also McClane, McClain

McLeaming, Daniel
   CA:177, 183, 184, 186, 221, 222, 224, 226, 228, 234, 332
   MA:167, 175
   See also Leaming

McLean, William
   CA:417, 418
   JA:73
   MA:499

McMillan, John
   CA:51
   JA:9, 54, 74
   MA:216, 234, 291, 314, 501, 502
   See also Millen

McMillen, John
   JA:40, 108, 109
   MA:380
   See also Millen

McMillion, Jno./John CA:289, 290, 295, 414
McMillion, Mina CA:290, 292, 293 See also Millen

McMillon, John MA:225McMillon, John sig mark MA:82
See also Millen

McPatterson, William JA:113

Meeker, Clark JA:138
Meeker, Daniel
   CA:323, 361, 419, 506, 507, 532, 546-552
   JA:63, 74, 85, 98, 103, 104, 114, 136, 162
   MA:417, 449, 500

Mellin, Charles JA:202

Melville, Andrew
   CA:1, 2
   JA:1
   MA:7
Melville, John
   CA:1, 2
   JA:1
   MA:7

Meriam, Charles admr JA:130

Merriam, Abner W. estate JA:130

Merry, Daniel MA:116

Merryfield & Hanna MA:326

Merryfield & Hannah
 CA:243-246, 282-284, 298, 300, 301, 315-317, 320, 365-367, 374-379, 394, 396, 398, 401, 426, 432, 446, 447, 486, 487, 497, 572
 JA:52
 MA:206(2), 251, 327, 373, 375
Merryfield & Sample CA:191
Merryfield CA:188, 189, 197, 199
Merryfield, Hannah & Liston CA:581
Merryfield, R.
 [MA:527]
 CA:267
 JA:11, 30, 128
Merryfield, R. sig JA:120
Merryfield, Robert MA:107
Merryfield, Roberts
 CA:151, 246, 369, 426
 JA:22, 52, 108, 117
 MA:59, 89, 196, 249
Merryfield, Roberts bail MA:178

Michigan Bank CA:508

Michigan City
 CA:53, 188-192, 255, 318, 320, 338, 339, 342, 360, 374, 378, 499, 503, 512, 513, 515, 520-522, 526, 529, 547, 569, 572, 578, 584
 JA:85
 MA:253, 507

Michigan City Gazette
  CA:297 MA:313, 328, 367
Michigan Road CA:559
Michigan Township CA:52, 53

Millen, Mina M. CA:466
See also McMillan, McMillen, McMillon, McMillion

Miller (Hiller?), Abraham JA:32
Miller, David MA:50
Miller, Isaac JA:153
Miller, Jacob
  CA:528
  JA:95
  MA:461, 482
Miller, Jacob associate judge
  CA:1
  MA:13, 25
Miller, Jacob judge MA:1
Miller, Jacob judge sig MA:11
Miller, Noah JA:91
Miller, S. et al. JA:14
Miller, Samuel
  CA:192, 517, 525-527
  JA:25, 108, 112, 129, 136, 140, 148, 153
  MA:50, 119, 173, 192
Miller, Worrice CA:528

Millit, Jesse [crossed out] MA:2

Mills/Miller?, Samuel MA:118

Minor, C. L. CA:548, 550
Minor, Orin J. JA:144

Mixon, James MA:12

Molton, Jonathan
  CA:16
  MA:31

Monday, Reuben
  CA:532
  JA:90
Monday, Reuben constable CA:251, 265, 404
See also Munday

Monger, Gaius JA:146

Mongoquenong/Monogoquonong village CA:18, 41

Monroe Circuit Court JA:6
Monroe County Circuit Court MA:168
Monroe County Library JA:6

Monson, Matilda CA:207

Montgomery County
  CA:45
  MA:30

Moon, Samuel JA:66

Moore, John S. MA:59, 100
Moore, Samuel
   CA:194, 195, 376
   MA:459

More, John S. CA:35

Morgan, Francis JA:140, 146, 157
Morgan, Isaac
   CA:68, 70-86, 88-112, 145, 146, 148-157, 159-166, 168, 169, 171, 172, 175, 176, 178, 179, 217, 219, 229, 231
   MA:50, 100
Morgan, Jesse
   CA:185, 192, 259, 416
   JA:41, 45, 73
   MA:120, 124, 229, 232, 234, 318, 340, 498
Morgan, John
   CA:62, 116, 137, 141, 557
   MA:50, 103, 122, 128, 129, 132, 159
Morgan, Johnathan MA:205
Morgan, Jonathan
   CA:23, 174, 181, 182, 184
   MA:4, 166, 208, 213, 220, 228
Morgan, Luther JA:152
Morgan, Newton JA:166, 167

Morrison, Alexander F. [crossed out] MA:454

Morrison, Alexander F. CA:422-424
   JA:75
   MA:508, 518
Morrison, E. MA:521
Morrison, E. admr. JA:196
Morrison, E. sig JA:118
Morrison, Erhart sig JA:119
Morrison/Morison, Ezekiel
   CA:369, 464, 532, 568
   JA:65, 104, 135, 188
   MA:452, 521
Morrison, Ezekiel sig JA:116
Morrison/Morison, R. S.
   CA:131
   JA:9, 14
   MA:99, 121, 160
Morrison/Morison, Robert L. CA:187, 222
Morrison/Morison, Robert L. deceased MA:392
Morrison, Robert S. [crossed out] MA:102
Morrison/Morison, Robert S.
   CA:62, 104, 116, 141, 177, 182-186, 221, 222, 224-226, 228, 234, 240, 266, 323, 332, 333, 557
   JA:20, 33
   MA:50, 89, 108, 122, 128, 129, 153, 159, 175, 239, 289, 321, 327, 334, 363, 364, 376 441, 447
Morrison/Morison, Robert S. deceased
   CA:426
   MA:521

Morrison/Morison, Robert S. JP CA:30-33, 41, 46, 51, 138, 139, 210, 211, 251, 262, 395, 399, 432, 433, 451, 454, 475, 476
  MA:40, 168, 356, 516
Morrison, Thomas M.
  CA:425, 426
  JA:9, 76
  MA:82, 512

Morse, Abner
  JA:36
  MA:205, 240, 290
Morse, Oliver MA:163
Morse, Orra [crossed out] MA:41, 102
Morse, Orra
  JA:4
  MA:49, 49 ½, 95, 108
Morse, Orra/Ora et al.
  JA:25
  MA:190
Morse, William P.
  JA:71
  MA:482

Mossman/Mosman, George
  CA:100-103, 138, 235, 269, 381, 382
  JA:15, 16, 19, 20, 35, 38, 47, 68, 109, 126
  MA:71, 79, 112, 125, 133, 151-153, 158, 253, 282, 307, 311, 350, 469, 470

Mossman, George/Geo bail
　CA:134, 239, 296　JA:40, 98Mossman, George bail sig MA:132, 283, 314

Mouland, Charles CA:21
See also Mowlan, Mowland

Moulsby John MA:382

Moulton, Jonathan
　CA:17, 174-176
　JA:3, 28
　MA:37, 44, 45, 209, 210
　Moulton, Jonathan bail CA:167
　Moulton, Jonathan bail sig MA:202

Mowlan/Mowland, Charles
　CA:21, 22
　MA:6, 22, 39
See also Mouland

Muir, Archibald
　JA:72
　MA:484

Mulks, John
　CA:271-275, 461, 462, 464, 467, 494, 529, 541, 558, 563, 568, 583
　　JA:43, 116, 141
　　MA:50, 195, 289, 333, 383, 387, 388

Mulks, John bail JA:83
Mulks, William   CA:116, 137, 141, 497, 498, 557
    JA:83, 116, 141
    MA:50, 122, 128, 129, 132, 159

Munay Daniel CA:133

Muncey, Jeremiah bail JA:112, 115

Munch, Charles G. Shff Porter County JA:165

Muncil, Roswell MA:4

Muncy, Jeremiah CA:380

Munday, Reuben MA:378
Munday, Reuben bailiff MA:255, 349
Munday, Reuben constable MA:391-2, 521
Munday, Reuben deputy sheriff MA:525
See also Monday

Mundy, Phineas JA:107

Munger, Gaines/Gains
    MA:2, 12
    JA:198
Munger, Gaius bail CA:23
Munger, Gaius sig JA:93

Munsel, Roswell CA:15, 63-67 JA:65
  MA:54, 120, 130, 324, 453
Munsel, Roswil CA:371

Munsell, Patrick MA:239
Munsell, Roswell
  CA:61, 133, 173, 302, 313-316
  JA:44, 48, 49, 111
  MA:12, 28, 34, 38, 40, 42, 316, 335, 351, 359, 361

Munsill, Roswill CA:372

Murray & Cutler JA:13
Murray, D. JA:13
Murray, Daniel
  CA:15
  MA:38, 40, 42, 130
Murray, Daniel bail CA:32, 33
Murray, Daniel bail sig MA:65
Murray, John & c.
  MA:309(2), 322
  JA:42
  MA:124
Murray, Samuel MA:28

Murrey, Daniel bail CA:30

Murry, Daniel MA:12, 116
Murry, Daniel bail sig? MA:55

Murry, John [crossed out] MA:233
Murry, John & c. MA:339
Murry, John MA:236

Myers, Isabella/Issabella
  CA:208
  JA:32
Myers/Myres, Isabella/Issabella/Isabela divorce MA: 117, 126, 207, 235
Myers, John H.
  CA:208
  JA:32
Myers/Myres, John H. divorce
  CA:207
  MA:117, 126, 235

N

Nale, David? CA:414

Neal, Asahel
 CA:287, 288
 JA:45
 MA:345

Nealy/Nealey/Neely, Charles P.
 CA:45
 JA:8
 MA:40, 41, 45, 73, 77

Neave, Charles CA:366, 367
  JA:64
  MA:450, 451
Neave, H. C. CA:365
Neave, Thompson
  JA:64
  MA:450

Nelson, Joseph
  JA:13
  MA:116

Neul, Asahel [crossed out] MA:342

New Durham CA:343
New Durham Township CA:23
New York CA:456, 524

Newel, Elisha CA:329, 331, 334, 336, 338, 340, 342
Newel, Noah CA:321

Newell, Elisha
  CA:326, 328, 459
  JA:148
  MA:13, 232
Newell, Elisha bail CA:286, 287

Newell, Noah
　CA:62, 67, 177, 182-184, 186, 187, 201, 212, 213,
　221, 222, 224, 226, 228, 232, 234, 285-287, 317, 326,
　328, 329, 331, 332, 334, 336, 338, 340, 342, 414,
　458-460, 462-465
　JA:46
　MA:53, 96, 165, 175, 195, 223, 255, 310, 346, 347,
　359, 396
　Newell, Noah bail CA:461
　Newell?, S. E. CA:465

Newhall, Elisha
　CA:17, 49, 54, 192, 458, 465, 544, 545
　MA:4, 12, 44, 50, 63, 84, 90, 95, 99, 255, 325
　Newhall, Elisha bail
　　CA:49
　　MA:80, 347
　Newhall, Elisha sig JA:148
　Newhall, Noah
　　CA:123
　　JA:26, 30
　　MA:95

Newhouse, John [MA:527]
Newhouse, John G. bail JA:114

Newkirk, Benoni/Benona M.
　JA:141
　MA:167, 387, 388

Newland, P. CA:321

Nichols/Nicholas, Nathan B.
CA:14-16, 240
JA:3
MA:12, 38, 289
Nichols, Nathan B. JP CA:201

Niles CA:215
Niles & Colerick CA:115
Niles & Jernegan CA:560
Niles & Orton CA:568
Niles & Sample CA:137, 301, 557
Niles & Taylor CA:393
Niles Everts & Liston CA:534, 536, 539, 540
Niles Liston & Everts CA:537
Niles, J. B.
    CA:16, 17, 506, 563
    JA:84
    MA:39, 97, 329
Niles, J. R. sig JA:93, 99
Niles, Jno B.
    CA:136, 242, 248-250, 252, 253, 255, 256, 258, 271, 272, 275, 344, 346, 358, 362, 364, 382, 506, 507, 512, 514, 547, 552, 579, 590, 595
    JA:3, 5, 9, 22, 26, 40, 63-65, 68, 123, 163, 165, 167, 171, 174, 179, 197, 201
    MA:68, 134, 173, 249, 250, 254, 304, 497
Niles, Jno B. [on inserted paper] JA:123
Niles, Jno B. bail CA:144
Niles, Jno B. bail sig MA:90, 161
Niles, Jno B. sig JA:88, 96, 113, 116, 126, 154
Niles, John B. [crossed out] MA:102

Niles, John B. [inserted paper] JA:126
Niles, John B.
    CA:29-32, 40, 43, 45, 50, 54, 57, 58, 134, 235, 236, 241, 247, 254, 274, 343, 345, 357, 358, 361, 363, 371, 379-381, 383, 384, 412, 413, 431, 447, 448, 505, 511, 513, 546, 549, 561, 562, 578, 589, 594
    JA:46, 65, 109, 177
    MA:13, 25, 108, 301, 303, 327, 356, 373, 375, 427, 456, 468, 469-471, 479, 515
Niles, John B. bail
    CA:39
    MA:92
Niles, John B. exec JA:101
Niles, John B. guardian MA:494
Niles, John B. prosecutor MA:59
Niles, Nathaniel
    CA:209, 562
    JA:22
    MA:89, 211
Niles, Nath. bail CA:144
Niles, Nathaniel bailiff MA:54, 96, 100, 162, 175, 242
Niles, Nathaniel deceased
    CA:561, 563
    MA:447
Niles, Orton & Saxton CA:567, 568
Niles, Nathl bail sig MA:161

Nilsworth?, William JA:52

Niscon, James bail JA:1

Nixon/Hixon?, James constable CA:47
Nixon, James bail CA:6

Noble, Noah governor MA:174

Norris, Thomas
  CA:464
  MA:382

North Bend [now in Starke County?] CA:8

Northam, Asa JA:152

Nowlan, Charles JA:3
See also Mowlan

Nunchelle, Elisha CA:232

O

O'Harra, Edward CA:65, 66
O'Harra, Edward bail CA:64
O'Harra, Edward Sr. bail CA:66
O'Harra, Michael
  CA:64, 65
  MA:12

Oakman, Joseph
  CA:508-510, 513, 514, 525, 527, 578, 579
  JA:79, 83, 84, 108, 117, 121, 133, 193
  MA:519
Oakman, Joseph bail JA:63

Oakman, Joseph sig? MA:520

Ogden, Mahlon D. sig [inserted page] JA:138

Ohara, Michael MA:309

Oharra, Charles MA:169
Oharra, Edward
  JA:39, 62
  MA:309, 442
Oharra, Edward/Edw bail
  JA:11
  MA:105
Oharra, Michael
  JA:11, 39, 62
  MA:105, 442

Ohio CA:345, 486, 488, 490, 491

Olinger, George
  CA:464
  JA:199
Olinger, George bail CA:579
Olinger, George constable CA:194
Olinger, George sig JA:201
Olinger, Isaac JA:130
Olinger, Samuel
  JA:95
  MA:50
Olinger, Samuel JP CA:52, 53
See also Clinger

Oliver, Barkley
 CA:287
 MA:346
Oliver, John C.
 CA:193
 JA:120

Olvin?, Asa MA:310

Oram, Hiram CA:499

Ormsby, Martin P. JA:181

Orr, Genl. Joseph MA:12
Orr, Joseph
 CA:46, 49, 54, 464
 MA:50, 63, 73, 80, 84, 90, 382, 476
Orr, Joseph C.
 CA:174, 181-183, 462, 508-510, 578, 579
 JA:159
 MA:50, 166, 205, 208, 213, 220, 228
Orr, Joseph C. sig JA:79, 133, 139
Orr, Joshua CA:48

Orrin, Joshua CA:286

Orrs, Joseph C. JA:96

Orton & Saxton CA:580, 581
  JA:187
  MA:390
Orton, H. N. constable
  CA:140, 142, 210, 211
  MA:168
Orton, H. S. sig CA:132
Orton, Harlow N.
  CA:17
  MA:44
Orton, M. H.
  CA:269, 270, 276, 277, 280, 553-555
  JA:114, 199
  MA:250
Orton, M. H. sig JA:95, 136
Orton, Myron H.
  CA:281
  JA:190
  MA:301, 419

Orum & Russell CA:499, 572
Orum, Hiram ["& Russell" crossed out] JA:99
Orum, Hiram
  CA:498, 500, 572, 573
  JA:113

Orwell house CA:435

Osbon, A. L. sig. JA:175

Osborn, A. L. JA:130, 151, 172
Osborn, Joseph CA:49, 563

Osborne, Joseph MA:44

Osburn, Joseph CA:467

Overmeyer, Daniel CA:141 page attached

Overmyre, Solomon
  CA:54
  MA:50, 90
Overmyre, Solomon bail CA:83, 85
Overmyre, Solomon bail sig MA:143, 144

Owen/Owens, Asa
  CA:61, 63-67, 173, 461, 462, 495, 541, 558
  JA:40, 143, 196, 201
  MA:50, 54, 383
Owen, Edwin JA:147, 148, 175

P

Pagan, David JA:199
Pagan, Joseph MA:12, 28

Page, David [crossed out] JA:111
Page, David
  CA:18, 116, 144, 557
  JA:2, 3, 5, 13, 14, 128
  MA:20, 37, 50, 116, 119, 122, 128, 129, 161, 482
Page, David sig JA:111, 133
Page, Reed [crossed out] JA:111

Page, Reed/Reid
 CA:18
 JA:2, 3, 5, 13, 128, 133
 MA:20, 37, 116, 482
Page, Wilder
 CA:46, 49, 50, 63, 73, 80, 84, 95

Pain, Erastus CA:17
See also Payne

Parker, John C. CA:358
Parker, Miller
 CA:280, 282
 JA:50
 MA:328, 367
Parker, Theron
 CA:61, 63-67, 173
 MA:50, 54
Parker, William
 CA:323
 MA:355
Parker, William D.
 CA:321
 JA:48
 MA:354
Parker, William H. CA:323
Parker, William J. CA:323

Parrott, John MA:206(2)
Parsons, Elihu [crossed out] MA:6

Parsons, Elihu MA:3, 8, 19
Parsons, Solomon
   CA:21, 22, 152, 156, 158
   JA:3
   MA:6, 22, 39

Patee, Eliphalet JA:156

Patrick, Palmer JA:186

Patterson & Clarkson
   CA:363
   MA:449, 450
Patterson, Thomas B.
   CA:406
   MA:481
Patterson, William
   CA:363
   JA:42, 188
   MA:324
Patterson, William M.
   CA:364
   JA:64
   MA:449-450
Patterson, William M. bail CA:434
Patterson, William M. bail sig MA:438

Payne, Erastus MA:44, 95, 352
Payne, Erastus bail MA:89
See also Pain

Peak, Aaron JA:16

Pearce, M. CA:321
Pearce, Michael
  CA:415
  MA:492
Pearce, Peter CA:287, 312
See also Peirce, Pierce

Peck, Francis CA:132
Peck, Willys JA:92, 144, 147, 168
Peck, Willys bail JA:177, 180, 181, 197
See also Peek

Pecket, John A. JA:126

Peek, Doomes JA:128(2)
Peek, Francis
  CA:132
  JA:159
See also Peck

Peirce, Peter MA:346
See also Pearce, Pierce

Pellet, William C.
  CA:594
  JA:81, 103

Pence, Peter
   CA:323   MA:99, 373
Pence, Peter bail CA:383
Pence, Peter bail sig MA:470
Pence, Peter bailiff MA:517

Pendell/Pendill, James P.
   CA:131
   JA:151, 164

Penin/Pennin, Joseph judge in Ohio CA:488, 490

Penwell, George bail CA:48
Penwell, George bail sig MA:75

Pepper, William
   CA:184, 233, 234, 323, 324
   JA:48
   MA:277, 278, 357, 358
Pepper, William bail
   CA:184
   MA:231

Perkins, Jeremiah
   CA:278
   JA:49
   MA:322, 365
Perkins, Jeremiah bail MA:366
Perkins, Susannah CA:278

Peters, Hans naturalization MA:244

Pettis, Samuel CA:532

Peyton, Francis JA:145

Phelps, Isaac N. JA:155

Phenix Bank JA:168

Philadelphia CA:413

Philips, Nimrod JA:142
Philips, Thomas H.
  CA:378
  JA:123, 136, 138, 202
  MA:460, 524
Philips, Thomas H. sig JA:66
Philips/Phillips, William
  CA:1, 501
  JA:49, 144
  MA:166, 316, 351, 361
Philips/Phillips, Wm. sig JA:84, 171

Picket, John A. JA:171

Pierce, Jesse, constable CA:193
Pierce, Michael
  CA:427
  MA:512

Pierce, Warner
   CA:146, 147
   JA:23
   MA:176
Pierce, Warren
   JA:39
   MA:308
   See also Pearce, Peirce

Pikens, Jeremiah MA:488, 489

Piles, David
   CA:68
   MA:107, 179

Place & Tharp CA:47
Place & Tharpe [crossed out] JA:8
Place & Tharpe
   JA:5
   MA:69, 75
Place, Wilder A. CA:84
Place, Willard A. CA:68, 70-83, 85, 86, 88-112, 145, 146, 148-151, 153-157, 159-166, 168, 169, 171, 172, 175, 176, 178, 179, 217, 219, 229
Place, Willard S. CA:231
Place, William/Willis? H. MA:50

Plainfield CA:387, 390, 391
Plainfield, St. Joseph County, Indiana CA:559

Platt, Ezra JA:119

Pleasant Township CA:251

Pleasants, Caleb E.
  CA:383
  JA:69
  MA:471

Plymate, Bowing
  CA:60, 61
  JA:10
  MA:60, 101, 102, 134
Plymate, John B. MA:52, 78

Polke, A. G.
  CA:297
  JA:49
  MA:171
Polke, A. G. bail
  CA:144
  JA:1
Polke, A. G. bail sig MA:161
Polke, Adam G. MA:174, 208, 362, 378, 431
Polke/Polk, Adam G. bail
  CA:5, 15, 16, 111, 112, 166, 170-172, 347, 542
  MA:15, 38, 156, 157, 201, 207
Polke/Polk, Adam G. bail sig MA:426
Polke/Polk, Adam G. sheriff MA:1, 2, 13, 25, 53, 100, 255
Polke, Adam G. sig JA:115

Pool, John CA:46
MA:12, 50, 63, 73, 84, 85, 382

Porter & Clark JA:101
Porter County
  CA:280
  JA:145
  MA:319
Porter, W. JA:139

Posey, Thomas MA:123

Post Boy schooner CA:188-190, 192

Power, Jonathan M. MA:29

Powers, David
  CA:68, 70-86, 88-112, 145, 146, 158-151, 153-157, 159-166, 168, 169, 171, 172, 175, 176, 178, 179, 217, 219, 229, 231
  JA:142
  MA:50, 100
Powers, J. W. CA:44
Powers, Jonathan JA:8
Powers, Jonathan W.
  CA:44, 45
  MA:30, 69

Prater Thomas JA:171

Pratt, Horace CA:321
President and trustees of the Town of La Porte
  CA:409
  JA:72, 188
  MA:485

Preston JA:113

Price, Samuel Z. bail CA:595

Prime, N. CA:437
Prime, Nathaniel
  CA:436, 438, 440-444
  JA:58
  MA:197-200, 266, 267, 424

Prosser?, Nathan JA:144

Provalt, Ezekiel CA:277

Provancil, Alexander MA:20
See also Provoncil

Provolt, Ezekiel
  CA:13, 15, 17, 225, 227, 230, 282, 287, 302, 312, 317
  MA:4, 12, 27, 34, 38, 40, 42, 44, 47, 167, 275, 279, 283, 322, 335, 346, 359, 365-367, 373

Provoncil, Alexander
  CA:20 MA:21
Provoncil, Alexis JA:2
See also Provancil

Provoncile/Provoncille, Alexander MA:33, 36
Provoncile, Alexis MA:26

Pruddell, Henry bail JA:109

Public Square CA:543

Quinlan, Michael JA:176

Quivey/Quivy, Erastus
　CA:62, 116, 137, 557
　MA:50, 103, 122, 128, 129, 132

R

Rahway CA:256, 257

Rambo/Ramboo, Absalom
  CA:240, 265, 322
  JA:75
  MA:4, 12, 289, 354, 355, 506
Rambo, Adonijah MA:205

Randolph County CA:207

Ransom, Wooden et al. JA:151

Rathbun, Daniel D.
  CA:464
  JA:42, 109
  MA:321, 322, 382

Rathbun, Daniel D. & others JA:178Rathbun, J. CA: 490
Rathbun, John
  CA:486, 489
  JA:102
  MA:293

Rathburn, D. CA:323, 324
Rathburn, John MA:437

Rathun, J. CA:488

Ray, Martin M. MA:2

Read, John C. MA:382

Redding, Benjamin JA:108
Redding, John
  CA:46, 48, 182, 183, 203, 232, 326, 327, 329, 331, 334, 336, 338, 340, 342, 458, 459, 465
  MA:1, 12, 28, 167, 228, 255

Reed, Daniel MA:382
Reed, George W. MA:93
Reed, Horwell CA:559
Reed, Isaiah
  CA:185, 247, 394, 396-402, 406
  MA:206, 206(2), 225, 229, 236, 299, 332, 474, 475, 481
Reed, Isaiah & wife JA:43, 69

Reed, Jarusha/Jerusha, Isaiah's wife   CA:397-402
    MA:206, 225, 236, 309(2), 332, 475
Reed, John C.
    CA:464
    MA:515
Reed, Joseph
    CA:23, 544, 545
    MA:325

Reeves & McLean
    CA:417, 418
    MA:499
Reeves, John
    CA:417, 418
    JA:73
    MA:499

Reid, George W. MA:93(2), 110, 121
Reid, Isaiah MA:309(2)

Replogle, Jacob
    CA:479
    JA:82

Reprogle, Jacob
    CA:177, 182-184, 186, 187, 221, 222, 224, 226, 228, 234, 332
    MA:175

Resnogle, Jacob MA:166

Revel, Isaiah JA:53

Reynolds, John
  CA:83, 84, 180
  JA:17, 181
  MA:143, 144
Reynolds, Joseph
  JA:46
  MA:206(2), 226, 242, 310, 323, 345
Reynolds, William F. JA:164

Rhinehart, John bail JA:192

Rhodes, Benjamin naturalization MA:523
Rhodes, Jonas naturalization MA:522

Ricardson, Ira CA:161

Rice, Ica F.
  CA:180, 231
  JA:35, 36
  MA:261-263, 284-286
Rice, Ira F. MA:187
Rice, Jacob MA:40, 188
Rice, Luther
  CA:480, 482
  MA:452
Rice, Moses bail
  CA:232
  JA:36
  MA:284-286

Rice, Vicory JA:93

Richards, John R. sig JA:186

Richardson, Andrew
  CA:173
  JA:107
  MA:383
Richardson, Edmund MA:514
Richardson, Ira
  CA:68, 70-86, 88-112, 145, 146, 148-151, 153-157, 159, 160, 162-166, 168, 169, 171, 172, 175, 176, 178, 179, 217, 219, 229, 231
  MA:50, 100
Richardson, Likins MA:514

Richmond
  CA:303
  MA:170

Ring, John [crossed out] MA:65
Ring, Victor [crossed out] MA:65

Rinker, Henry
  CA:62, 133, 137, 141, 168, 349
  JA:27, 61
  MA:50, 103, 130, 132, 159, 202, 312, 525
Rinker, Henry bail
  CA:147
  MA:176

Rinker, Joseph CA:133
  MA:130
Rinker, Joseph bail
  CA:181
  MA:227

Rinott, John JA:28

Robb, David [CA:0 – apparently a misplaced page from April 1835]
Robb, David [crossed out] MA:135
Robb, David
  CA:24, 46, 48, 68-112, 145-172, 175, 176, 178-180, 217-220, 229-231, 323, 394, 436
  MA:48, 50, 100
Robb, David, Major CA:395, 400

Robertson, Daniel JA:186
Robertson, Jacob A. JA:151
Robertson, Lemuel MA:50

Robinson, Alexander H. or A. H. sig JA:146
Robinson, Elisha J.
  CA:435
  JA:76
  MA:512
Robinson, Elisha S. CA:434

Robinson, Hezekiah
 CA:337, 393, 405, 415, 426   MA:382, 435, 442, 455, 461, 480, 485, 492, 503, 512
Robinson, Lemuel
 CA:23, 61, 63, 173
 JA:171
 MA:54
Robinson, Samuel CA:64-67
Robinson, William CA:23
Robinson, William bail
 CA:345
 MA:416
Robinson, Wm. W. JA:191

Robison, D. CA:321
Robison, Hezekiah CA:410

Rockhill, J. E. CA:286
Rockhill, Joel
 CA:185
 MA:229

Rodgers, Isaac JA:200

Rodifa, H. CA:321

Rogers, Aquilla W. CA:321
Rogers, Aquilla W. JP CA:404, 405
Rogers, David JA:129

Root, Josiah
  CA:141 page attached
  JA:106, 189
  MA:382
Rose, D. G. CA:380
Rose, D. G. sig JA:191
Rose, G. A. CA:323
Rose, Gilbert MA:372
Rose, Gustavus A. CA:458
Rose, Jacob MA:213

Ross, Abner
  JA:94
  MA:462
Ross, Abner S. JA:184
Ross, James [crossed out] MA:342
Ross, James
  CA:287, 288
  JA:45
  MA:345
Ross, John D.
  CA:414, 460, 462, 463
  MA:382, 396, 419
Ross, W. C. JA:90
Ross, W. O. CA:126

Ross, William O. [crossed out] MA:217

Ross, William O.   CA:11, 14, 42, 47, 52, 122-125, 131, 207, 286, 310, 349, 352, 368, 411, 417, 418
   JA:5, 6, 13, 50, 54, 55, 61, 62
   MA:2, 13, 24, 48, 67, 121, 301, 393, 419, 439, 486, 499, 515Ross, William O. bail
   CA:22   MA:58
Ross, William O. bail sig MA:39
Ross, William O. JP
   CA:49, 51, 54, 57-59, 129, 130, 138, 143, 201, 203, 208-210, 239, 240, 259-261, 267, 286, 321, 322, 324, 347, 348, 350, 351, 353, 355, 370, 403, 404, 406-410, 416, 419-421, 425, 426, 431, 432
   MA:50(2), 51, 164, 165, 244(2), 245, 246, 251, 253, 381, 392
Ross, William O. master in chancery MA:242
Ross, William O. sig [overwritten across page] MA:75
Ross, William P. MA:115

Rucker, Ambrose
   CA:232, 298, 300, 301, 322, 326, 328, 329, 331, 334, 336, 338, 340, 342, 458, 459, 465
   JA:44, 75
   MA:215, 218, 225, 255, 291, 309(2), 335, 340, 342, 352, 355, 360, 363, 476, 506
Rucker, Ambrose sig JA:156
Rucker, Henry MA:439

Rudiffer, Harrison bailiff CA:467

Rue & Lindsey JA:45Rue, Abraham MA:104, 179, 256, 397
Rue, Isaiah MA:235
Rue, Jacob
   CA:45, 67, 68, 145, 164, 179-181, 203, 226, 323, 324, 385-387, 389-393
   JA:8, 12, 23, 25, 34, 39, 59, 70
   MA:41, 73, 77, 112, 176, 227, 279, 280, 306, 308, 331, 341, 428, 442, 443
Rue, Jacob bail MA:230
Rue, Jacob et al. bail JA:31

Rush & Hubbill
   CA:480-483, 485
   JA:87, 93
   MA:452
Rush, H. JA:87, 93
Rush, Hiram
   CA:480, 482
   MA:452
Rush, John admr JA:156
Rush, Mathew admr JA:156

Russel/Russell, Ebenezer
   CA:62, 116, 137, 141, 144, 557
   MA:50, 103, 122, 128, 129, 132, 159, 161

Russell, Chester G. JA:172, 193
Russell, Chester G., [crossed out] JA:127
Russell, John CA:50, 498, 500, 572
Russell, Sylvanus JA:184
Russell, William JA:134

S

S. F. Dorr & Co. JA:173

Sack [Sauk?] Trace CA:559

Safford, Ephraim CA:172

Sail, Thomas W. MA:205

Sailor, Benjamin CA:6
See also Salor, Saylor

Sale, Darius MA:382, 396

Sale, Derias CA:460, 462, 463
Sale, Thomas N. MA:213
Sale, Thomas W.
   CA:181, 182, 192
   MA:166, 208, 220, 228, 232, 289

Sallicutt?/Syllicutt? [written over], Sylvia CA:55

Salor, Benjamin CA:7
Salor, John CA:561
See also Sailor, Saylor

Salsbury, Nelson MA:167

Salyer, G. Z. CA:45
Salyer, George L. MA:158
Salyer, George Z.
   CA:48, 79, 357, 403, 471-474
   JA:25, 39, 41, 63, 68, 71, 79
   MA:95, 193, 273, 274, 310, 318, 431, 447, 469, 480
Salyer, George Z. bail
   CA:78, 181
   MA:227
Salyer, George Z. bail sig MA:141
Salyer, George Z. bailiff MA:96

Sample & Liston
   CA:44
   MA:29
Sample & McGaffery CA:19

Sample & Niles CA:301
Sample, S. C.
　CA:7
　JA:29, 45
　MA:39, 342
Sample, S. C. bail JA:18
Sample, Samuel bail CA:86
Sample, Samuel C.
　CA:6, 44, 126, 128
　MA:2, 13, 14, 133, 136
Sample, Samuel C. bail
　CA:21
　MA:33, 144
Sample, Samuel C. judge MA:396
Sample, Samuel C. prosecutor
　CA:34, 61
　MA:56, 100, 176, 256

Sanford, Adaline/Adeline
　JA:72
　MA:391, 485
Sanford, Adaline's father MA:391, 485
Sanford, George
　JA:72
　MA:391, 484
Sanford, Rachel, George's wife
　JA:72
　MA:391, 484

Saxton/Jackson??, Morice W. MA:419

Saxton, N. W. [MA:527]
Saxton, Norris W. JA:157, 161

Saylor, Benjamin
    CA:149, 177, 182-187
    JA:23
    MA:175, 177, 217
Saylor, John
    CA:561, 562
    JA:101
    MA:447
Saylor, John bail JA:109
See also Sailor, Salor

Scales, L. sig JA:102

Scarce, Samuel
    JA:56
    MA:270, 271
See also Seaver

Scare?, Samuel MA:410

Scele, Thomas W. CA:174

Schank, Isaac
    CA:296, 297
    JA:40
    MA:313

Scipio Township
   CA:1, 141, 142, 200, 239, 276, 314, 315

Scott, James CA:165, 166
Scott, James M.
   CA:165, 468
   JA:27, 80, 114, 147, 174, 177, 180, 181, 197
   MA:191, 200, 201, 382, 491
Scott, M. Warren JA:161
Scott, Samuel JA:147, 174, 181, 197
Scott, Samuel bail JA:114
Scott, William [crossed out] MA:216
Scott, William
   JA:44, 101
   MA:221, 339
Scott, William and another MA:489

Seargeant, John MA:177, 179

Sears, William JA:134

Seaver?/Scarce?, Saml. E. bail JA:180

Seff?/Self?, Joseph B. CA:532

Seffins, George bail CA:591

Selcregg, George JA:103
See also Selkregg, Silkregg

Self, J. B. Jr. CA:321
Self, Joseph B. or J. B. sig JA:121

Selkregg, Nelson JA:135
See also Selcregg, Silkregg

Seminary Trustee JA:1-3, 6, 7, 9-12, 15-21, 23-25, 28, 29, 31, 32, 34, 36, 48, 50, 57, 59-61, 63, 70, 73, 78-83, 92, 103, 106, 107, 117, 134, 153, 160

Sergeant, John
  CA:148
  MA:260, 265

Sering, John
  CA:578, 579
  JA:96

Serrill Bernard & Co. CA:413
Serrill, Pearson
  CA:412, 413
  JA:69

Seymore, James JA:167, 198

Shadney, John B. MA:35

Shalabarger, Isaac
  CA:262
  JA:46
  MA:348

Shandonnois, John Baptist MA:75
See also Chandonnois

Shandy, Israel
 CA:125, 126
 JA:13
 MA:115, 171

Sharpless, Avery CA:42

Shase, William C. JA:92

Shaw, Andrew
 CA:329, 330
 JA:57
 MA:415

Shaw, Levi C.
 CA:372, 373
 JA:65
 MA:456, 457

Shaw, Thomas
 JA:32
 MA:76, 84, 85, 87, 93(2), 125, 233, 238

Sheagley, Saml. JA:180

Shedd & Turner JA:147, 157, 175, 177, 183

Sheldon, James JA:155

Shell, Joseph CA:60

Sheridan/Sheriden/Sheridon, William
    CA:139, 409
    JA:56
    MA:276, 411

Sherr, Henry Jr. JA:12

Sherwood, Jeremiah
    MA:12, 25, 383
    JA:100
Sherwood, John
    JA:38, 130, 151
    MA:306
Sherwood, Jonathan
    CA:227, 263, 264
    JA:47
    MA:2, 279, 324, 354

Shew, Henry MA:157
Shew, Henry Jr. MA:114

Shields, James JA:127

Shimmin, William
    CA:467
    JA:92

Shimmin, William naturalization
    CA:456, 457
    MA:70, 509

Shirley/Shirly, Lewis
    CA:16, 17, 321, 323
    JA:3, 48
    MA:31, 37, 44, 45, 354, 355

Shirtleff & Williams [crossed out] MA:458
Shirtleff, Oliver
    CA:286
    JA:65, 69
    MA:455

Shirtliff, Oliver [crossed out]
    JA:115
    MA:458
Shirtliff/Shirliff, Oliver
    CA:209, 323, 324, 335, 337, 369, 370, 379, 380, 393, 406, 410, 422, 427, 430
    JA:68
    MA:382, 435, 437, 442, 502

Shoemaker, William JA:182

Shotwell, Eden
    JA:72
    MA:382, 390, 485

Shoufler, William C. MA:135

Shurte, Samuel bail sig MA:7

Shurtliff & Williams MA:472
Shurtliff/Shurtliffe, Oliver MA:452, 468, 472, 481, 485, 512, 515

Silkregg, George
   CA:193
   MA:383
See also Selcregg, Selkregg

Silver/Silvers, Elizabeth
   CA:8, 9
   JA:2
   MA:3, 6, 18, 22, 133
   Silver, James T. CA:9

Simpkins, Silas
   CA:262
   MA:348

Simpson, Nathan MA:179, 256
Simpson, Solomon CA:479, 480

Sinclair, David CA:290

Singleton CA:559

Sinner, Henry C. JA:183

Sirrell Bernard & Co. CA:412

Skillman, Isaac N. MA:243

Skinner & Finley [crossed out] MA:457
Skinner & Finley
  CA:419
  JA:74
  MA:417
Skinner, H. C.
  JA:27
  MA:206
Skinner, Henry C.
  CA:360
  JA:63, 110
  MA:448, 519
Skinner, Mr. CA:194

Slater?, Jacob JA:122

Sleight & Moore JA:173

Small, William JA:143, 173

Smallwood, Bennet MA:441
Smallwood, Bennet sig mark MA:384
Smallwood, Burnett MA:327

Smallwood, Samuel
   CA:33, 34, 251
   JA:6, 53
   MA:57, 300, 315, 321, 327, 334, 376, 384, 441, 447

Smith, Elias B. [crossed out] JA:8
Smith, Elias B.
   CA:41
   JA:6
   MA:76
Smith, Ensign B.
   CA:16, 17, 23
   JA:3, 4
   MA:31, 37, 44, 45, 47
Smith, Erastus MA:274, 400
Smith, James F.
   CA:464
   MA:126
Smith, James F. bail CA:482, 485
Smith, James H. JA:90
Smith, John N. JA:150
Smith, Julius MA:383
Smith, Richard CA:141 page attached
Smith, Robert JA:148
Smith, Samuel JA:197
Smith, Silas
   CA:501-504
   JA:84, 85, 120, 122, 183
Smith, Walter JA:121
Smith, White B. CA:435

Snider, Isaac CA:276, 323
Snider, Mr. CA:193

Snodgrass, William MA:243

Snow & Welker JA:62
Snow, Thomas
  JA:130, 186
  MA:320, 395, 443

Snyder, Isaac
  CA:335-337
  JA:50, 67
  MA:366, 369, 422, 430, 435, 465
Snyder, Isaac bail MA:370
Snyder, James JA:146, 165

Sorrill Bernard & Co. MA:470
Sorrill, Pearson MA:470

South Bend CA:24, 25, 45, 484

Southerland, William JA:114

Southmayd, Timothy JA:137

Southwood, William JA:97

Spalding/Spaulding, William
  CA:322
  MA:355

Speaks, Aaron
  CA:138
  MA:133, 158

Speirs, Daniel CA:193

Spencer, James [MA:527]
Spencer, James
  JA:50, 91
  MA:360, 365

Spitz, John CA:133

Sprague, D. bail JA:88, 111
Sprague, Daniel CA:339
Sprague/Sprage, David
  CA:131, 170, 193, 306, 308-310, 318, 326, 338, 342, 376, 569
  JA:27, 36, 39, 45, 60, 65, 86, 119, 122, 143, 164, 173, 182, 185, 189, 191
  MA:166, 205(2), 206, 230, 241, 250, 271, 287, 290, 294, 308, 316, 335, 344, 349, 385, 405, 406, 433, 434, 455, 505, 519
Sprague/Sprage, David bail
  JA:63, 84, 88, 89, 116, 172
  MA:458
Sprague, David sig? MA:520

Sprague, Teall & Co. JA:126

Springfield, Ohio CA:486, 488, 490

Spurlock, Burwell CA:321
Spurlock, Burwell bail
  CA:313, 358, 409
  JA:150
  MA:448
Spurlock, Burwell bail sig MA:373, 490
Spurlock, Cyrus MA:166

St. Clair, Arthur
  CA:516
  JA:84, 172
St. Clair, David
  CA:289, 295, 465, 466
  JA:40, 74
  MA:12, 216, 225, 234, 291, 314, 501, 514

St. James & Clark JA:102

St. Joseph County
  CA:56, 137, 240, 484
  MA:160, 173, 238
St. Joseph County, Michigan CA:582
St. Joseph County, Michigan Territory
  CA:457, 528
  MA:509

Stanfield, Eli [crossed out] JA:59

Stanfield, Eli   CA:185, 203, 347, 348, 461, 462
  JA:55, 83
  MA:17, 229, 380, 381, 426

Stanton, Aaron
  CA:61, 63-67, 173, 177, 182-184, 186, 187, 221, 222, 224, 401, 402, 589, 590
  MA:2, 12, 54, 108, 175, 289, 515
Stanton, Aaron sig JA:96
Stanton, Albert
  CA:13
  MA:27
Stanton, Alfred
  MA:12, 34, 40, 382
Stanton, Alfred sig JA:116
Stanton, Elijah MA:2
Stanton, John
  MA:12, 13, 167, 275, 279, 283, 322, 335, 346, 351, 354, 359, 365-367, 373
Stanton, Joseph MA:382
Stanton, Morrice W. MA:419
Stanton, Thomas E. MA:456
See also Staunton

Starling, Benjamin JA:129

Starr, Buel JA:42
Starr, Chandler CA:522
Starr, Ruel MA:325

Starrett, Joseph JA:107

Starrs, Chandler JA:89

Startman, William JA:44

State Bank of Illinois CA:515

Staunton, Aaron [crossed out] MA:102
Staunton, Aaron
   CA:226, 228, 234, 240, 321, 332, 397, 415, 430
   MA:14, 492
Staunton, Alfred
   CA:49
   MA:44
Staunton, John
   CA:49, 225, 227, 230, 265, 277, 281, 287, 302, 312, 317, 323
   MA:2, 44
Staunton, William MA:2
See also Stanton

Steel/Steele, Nathaniel
   CA:260, 261
   JA:46
   MA:347

Steenbergen, John B.
  CA:533-535, 541
  JA:98, 99

Stephen, Andrew D.
  JA:28
  MA:206(2)

Stephens, Benjamin Jr. JA:194
Stephens, Charles JA:81, 121

Sterling, Benjamin JA:92
Sterling, Sarah MA:241, 272, 287, 288

Sterrett, Joseph MA:383

Steurt, Robert bail CA:374

Stevens, Charles bail [crossed out] MA:514
Stevens, Charles
  JA:39, 42
  MA:307, 324, 473
Stevens, Charles bail
  CA:68
  JA:12
  MA:112
Stevens, Gilbert MA:135
Stevens, James B. CA:321
Stevens, Walter
  JA:47
  MA:348

Steward, R. bail JA:85

Stewart & Andrews JA:168
Stewart JA:137
Stewart, R. CA:501, 503
Stewart, R. bail
  CA:374
  JA:66
Stewart, Robert [crossed out] JA:116
Stewart, Robert
  CA:131, 501, 503
  JA:66, 84-86, 97 108, 118, 121, 143, 156, 162, 179, 181, 191
  MA:460, 524
Stewart, Robert bail JA:89
Stewart, Robert bail sig MA:457
Stewart, Samuel JA:157, 161

Stilson, Leonard MA:267, 400

Stilwell, Richard JA:147

Stinson and Finley MA:500

Stocking, Samuel JA:133

Stockwell, Nathan H. JA:164

Stoner, David
  JA:102
  MA:351

Stout, Aquilla S. JA:125
Stout, John
  CA:48
  MA:99

Stover, George
  JA:35
  MA:283
Stover, George bail CA:237
Stover, George bail sig MA:282
Stover, George E. MA:515
Stover, George G. MA:455
Stover, George L. CA:337
Stover, George S.
  CA:238, 335, 393, 405, 415, 417, 427, 430
  JA:149
  MA:382, 436, 437, 442, 461, 480, 492, 498, 512
Stover, George S. bail CA:285
Stover, George S. bail sig MA:362

Strong, Harvey
  JA:37, 55, 90, 186
  MA:214, 249, 292, 391, 516
Strong, Harvey et al. JA:172

Sutton, William
 CA:34, 35   JA:6
 MA:58
Sutton, William bail
 CA:7
 JA:1
 MA:20

Swaney, Lewis JA:128

Swartz, Michael CA:14

Swiney, Larkin B. S. JA:108, 117

Switzer, Henry E.
 JA:35
 MA:261, 263, 284, 285

Swope, Wilson
 CA:92, 203
 JA:18
 MA:147

T

Talbott, William
   JA:52
   MA:298, 343

Taylor & Liston CA:204, 206
Taylor & Sample CA:133
Taylor, B. B.
   CA:556
   JA:1
   MA:190
Taylor, Benjamin CA:221, 222, 224, 226, 228, 234, 332

Taylor, Burrell/Burwell B.
  CA:75-77, 208, 209
  JA:33
  MA:93, 139, 140, 160, 239, 240, 247, 248, 305, 442
Taylor, George JA:100
Taylor, George bail JA:130
Taylor, George L. CA:381, 382
Taylor, Ithream JA:185
Taylor, M. CA:193
Taylor, William
  CA:131, 141 page attached
  JA:108
Taylor, William W. JA:134

Teal, William [crossed out] MA:83
Teal, William
  CA:57-59
  MA:51, 77, 86, 130, 173, 214, 224, 232

Teall & Sprague JA:47, 144
Teall Sprague & Co. JA:130, 179
Teall, Sprague, Hartshorn, & Tuttle JA:164
Teall, William [crossed out] MA:83
Teall, William
  CA:133, 319, 569
  JA:9, 25, 36, 37, 88, 119, 125, 182
  MA:119, 192, 205, 249, 271, 272, 287, 290, 293, 305, 335, 349
Teall, William bail MA:241
Teall, William et al. JA:138

Teeple, J. CA:209
Teeple, James CA:333
Teeple, John CA:409
Teeple/Teeples, John P.
   CA:49, 337, 393, 405, 415, 427
   MA:44, 382, 435, 442, 455, 461, 480, 492, 502, 503, 512
Teeple, John S. CA:421

Templeton, J. CA:209
Templeton, John
   CA:162, 163, 323
   JA:25
   MA:186

Terrell, Thomas MA:343

Terryl, Thomas [crossed out] MA:463
Terryll, Thomas MA:419

Tharp, James CA:1

Thomas, G. clerk sig MA:37
Thomas, George clerk
   CA:2
   MA:1, 25, 53
Thomas, George clerk deceased MA:98
Thomas, George deceased MA:99, 108
Thomas, George B. clerk MA:13

Thomas, John
  CA:340, 341
  JA:61, 67
  MA:406, 407, 434, 435, 464
Thomas, William MA:2, 12

Thompson & wife JA:36
Thompson, Henry MA:206, 290
Thompson, James [crossed out] MA:228
Thompson, James
  CA:181-184, 224
  JA:31, 106, 142
  MA:216228, 231, 275
Thompson, Mary, Henry's wife MA:206, 290
Thompson, Neave CA:365

Thornburgh, Absalom JA:120

Thrall, William C. MA:4, 12

Thurman, Augustin L. JA:125

Tinker, William JA:118

Tinklepough, Hiram JA:197, 198

Tinner, David JA:11

Tirrell, T. CA:372

Titsworth, William MA:226, 297

Todd, Adam JA:160
Todd, Hiram taken suddenly sick MA:95
Todd, Hyram CA:46

Toland, Henry
   JA:66, 126
   MA:460

Tomilson, John CA:405

Tomlinson, John
   CA:528
   JA:95
   MA:480, 482

Tompkins, Robert
   CA:406
   MA:481

Toogood, William JA:127

Torbert/Torbet/Torbut, Anthony
   CA:200, 583, 585, 586
   JA:30, 95, 107, 192
   MA:222

Town of Liberty, Union County CA:365, 367

Townsend & Kinney JA:171

Traitbass/Tratebas/Tratebass/Trateboss, Eugene
   CA:446, 447
   MA:326, 373-375, 473, 514
Traitbass/Tratebas/Tratebass/Trateboss, Eugene
infant MA:327, 494
Traitbass/Tratebas/Tratebass/Trateboss,
Maria/Mariah
   CA:246
   JA:52
   MA:243, 298, 473, 514
Traitbass/Tratebas/Tratebass/Trateboss, Maria
deceased CA:446
Traitbass/Tratebas/Tratebass/Trateboss, Maurice
   MA:326
Traitbass/Tratebas/Tratebass/Trateboss, Maurice
deceased
   CA:446-449
   MA:243, 327, 373-375, 473, 494-496

Traver, John B. MA:210
Traver, John R.
   CA:178, 179
   JA:31
   MA:209, 226, 227

Treadway, Griffin
   CA:251
   JA:39
   MA:250, 308, 316, 382, 446, 447

Treadway, Griffin bail CA:333, 542
Treadway, Griffin sig JA:125

Treat, Samuel sig JA:143

Tredway, G. JA:63

Tricker, Aulden MA:255

Trinkle, William
  JA:52
  MA:297

Trowbridge, Charles D. JA:156
Truesdell, Henry JA:125, 150

Trustees of School Dist. &c. JA:172
Trustees of School District No. 8 Town 36 N. R3W
MA:482

Tryon, David
  CA:515
  JA:93

Tucker, Alden/Allden/Aulden
  CA:232, 326, 327, 329, 331, 334, 336, 338, 340, 342, 458, 459, 465
  MA:167, 318, 352
Tucker, Charles
  JA:78
  MA:403

Tunker, William MA:226

Turner, David
 CA:116, 117, 177, 182-184, 186, 187, 221, 222, 224, 226, 228, 234, 332
 MA:107, 175
Turner, Samuel
 CA:68, 70-86, 88-112, 145, 146, 148-151, 153-157, 159-166, 168-172, 175, 176, 178, 179, 217, 219, 229, 231, 265, 287, 312, 406, 415, 417
 JA:45
 MA:50, 100, 226, 341, 346, 354, 481, 492, 498
Turner, Thomas I. bailiff MA:316, 349

Tutt Tho H. JA:11

Tuttle, F. JA:182
Tuttle, Frederick JA:119
Tuttle, Frederick bail JA:138
Tuttle, Nelson JA:174

Tyler, Ezra
 CA:13, 15, 17, 23
 MA:12, 27, 34, 38, 40, 42, 44, 167, 280

Tyrrell & Osborn JA:125, 127, 151, 160
Tyrrell and Wright CA:519, 524
Tyrrell, T.
 CA:373, 528
 JA:65, 175

Tyrrell, T. sig JA:149
Tyrrell, Thomas
   JA:201
   MA:488
Tyrrell, Thomas court official MA:479

Tyswall, JA:85

U

Underwood, Benjamin MA:382
Underwood, John B. MA:79
Underwood, Joseph B.
  CA:212, 213, 215
  JA:30
  MA:71, 111, 113, 192, 222

Union County CA:365, 367

Usher, Andrew Jackson CA:262

IN COURT IN LA PORTE

Usher, Charles
   CA:262, 263
   JA:46
   MA:348

Utley, Sandford/Sanford MA:28, 521

V

V. & I./J. King
  JA:12
  CA:122
  MA:113

Vail, H. L. MA:3
Vail, H. P. bail JA:12
Vail, Henry B. MA:185
Vail, Henry L.
  CA:137, 138, 462
  MA:5, 132, 134

Vail, Henry P.
  CA:161
  MA:185
Vail, Henry P. bail
  CA:67
  MA:111
Vail, Henry S. MA:50
Vail, J. T. MA:3
Vail, John T.
  CA:10-14, 16
  MA:5, 12, 13, 23

Vale, Thomas W. CA:184

Van Dalsen, Samuel CA:587
See also Vandalsen, Vandalsem

Van Pelt, Sutton
  CA:225
  JA:14
Van Pelt, Sutton bail CA:468
Van Pelt, Sutton, sheriff MA:396
See also Vanpelt

Van Vilzer John JA:181

Vanander, Samuel MA:275, 401

Vance, Danl. "Sh of M'gomey County" JA:164

Vancleave, Mathias CA:546

Vandalsem, Eunice MA:123
Vandalsem, Eunice pension MA:122
Vandalsem, Henry deceased MA:122, 123
See also Van Dalsen

Vandalsen/Vandalson/Vandolson, Samuel
   CA:287, 588
   JA:78
   MA:346
See also Van Dalsen

Vanmetre, John MA:166

Vanpelt & Shippee JA:117
Vanpelt, Sutton
   MA:119, 275, 351, 383
VanPelt, Sutton sheriff MA:517
See also Van Pelt

Vanpool Rufus
   CA:48
   JA:38
   MA:307

Vanrensalaer, John C. JA:133
VanRensalaer, John JA:161

Vaughn/Vaughan, Thomas P.
  CA:37
  JA:9
  MA:91

Vermillion County MA:189, 264, 399

Vessel on the stocks at Michigan City JA:127

Viceroy, John bail CA:330

Vickery, John CA:464

Vickory, John MA:382

Vicory & Rice JA:87
Vicory, John
  CA:480, 482
  JA:115
  MA:452
Vicory, John bail MA:415

Viele, Lodwick A. JA:142

Vincent & Bahan JA:62

W

W. Allen & Co. JA:195
W. D. & J. Blake
  CA:50, 244, 245
  MA:71, 81, 311
W. D. & T. D. Jones JA:29
W. G. & G. W. Ewing JA:62

Waddell, James MA:194

Waddle, James
  CA:110, 194, 195
  JA:26
  MA:318, 382

Wakefield, Jesse
  CA:414, 460, 462, 463
  JA:140
  MA:396

Walcott, Levi MA:390, 485

Walker, Henry
  CA:464
  MA:382
Walker, James
  CA:227, 335
  MA:279, 437
Walker, John MA:267, 400
Walker, Samuel MA:9
Walker, William J. or W. J. sig JA:116, 180, 195

Walls, James MA:382

Walters/Watters?, Absalom bail MA:94
Walters, A. CA:46
Walters, Absalam/Abraham CA:48
Walters, Absalom
  JA:21
  MA:159
Walters, Absalom bail CA:40

Ward, Robert E. JA:201

Ward, Samuel   JA:128(2)
   MA:462

Warner & Shedd & Turner bail JA:84
Warner, Asa M. MA:512
Warner, David [crossed out] JA:92
Warner, David
   CA:378, 379, 519, 524, 525
   JA:66, 85, 89, 108, 120, 122, 128
   MA:460, 524

Warren & Shedd & Turner bail JA:85
Warren, Asa M.
   CA:337, 393, 405, 410, 415, 421, 427, 430
   MA:12, 382, 436, 437, 442, 455, 461, 480, 485, 492, 502, 503, 515

Warrener, E. M. CA:286

Warrick, J. CA:321

Warriner, Ella
   CA:368, 411, 412
   JA:72
   MA:452, 486
Warriner, Ella sig JA:64

Washington City CA:204, 205

Watson, George CA:81

Watson, Robert F. JA:31
  MA:224

Watts, Oscar JA:161

Wayne County MA:169, 170

Weaver, Balah
  JA:38
  MA:253, 307
Weaver, Charles CA:365
Weaver, Henry
  CA:464
  JA:103

Webb, George F.
  JA:40
  MA:311
Webb, John
  CA:417
  MA:498
Webb, John bailiff MA:517
Webb, Thomas
  CA:406
  MA:481
Webb, Thomas H. JA:117
Webb, Walter W. JA:142

Webster, Amos G. CA:414, 460, 462, 463 MA:382, 396
Webster, Asaph
 CA:430
 MA:515
Webster, James
 CA:335, 345, 346, 393, 405, 410, 415, 421, 427, 430
 JA:59
 MA:12, 382, 426, 437, 442, 455, 461, 480, 485, 492, 502, 503, 512, 515
Webster, Samuel
 CA:430
 MA:515

Welb, G. F. CA:257
Welb, George F. CA:256

Welch, William A. CA:203

Weller, Shepherd MA:395

Wells/Mills?, Sylvester CA:141 page attached

Wells & Enos
 CA:498, 499, 521, 569-571, 583, 585
 JA:87, 93, 95, 139, 146, 150, 157, 173, 174, 191
Wells Vanderwort & Co. JA:128(2)
Wells, Henry JA:124

Wells, J. R.   CA:318, 430, 554, 563
      JA:42, 73, 95Wells, J. R. admr JA:94
Wells, J. R. sig [inserted paper] JA:126
Wells, Jabez R. [crossed out] MA:457
Wells, Jabez R.
   CA:131, 520, 528, 570
   JA:55, 84, 87, 126, 141, 160, 182, 191
   MA:390, 487
Wells, Jabez R. or J. R. sig JA:139, 140, 142, 154
Wells, John
   CA:464
   MA:95, 382
Wells, R. W. MA:301
Wells, Reuben JA:185

Welsh, Calvin JA:100

Wendle, William MA:298

Wendon, James A. bail JA:110

Wendover, James A. JA:134, 160

West, Charles MA:12
West, John [crossed out] MA:488

West, John
CA:446-451 JA:143
MA:327, 375, 376, 494-496
West, John sig JA:143West, William JA:181

Weston, Samuel
CA:174, 181, 212
JA:26, 143
MA:195, 208, 213, 220

Wetherill, John B. CA:519

Wetmore, David MA:124, 233
Wetmore, David & c. MA:332, 339

Wheeler & Landon
JA:8
MA:43, 52, 80
Wheeler & Langdon CA:48
Wheeler, A. bail JA:196
Wheeler, Amzi L.
CA:587, 591, 592
JA:107, 119, 162
Wheeler, Amzi L. or A. L. sig JA:78, 98
Wheeler, H. & T. MA:164
Wheeler, H.
JA:14
MA:311

Wheeler, Hiram [crossed out] MA:102Wheeler, Hiram
   CA:80, 131, 235, 241, 485
Wheeler, Hiram bail
   CA:320
   JA:123
Wheeler, Hiram bail sig MA:349
Wheeler, Preserved CA:141 page attached
Wheeler, Solomon CA:48
Wheeler, Tolman/Tolmon
   CA:235, 241, 249, 252, 343, 361, 363, 371, 497
   JA:35, 41, 51, 57, 63-65, 83
   MA:52, 75, 80, 206, 251, 254, 282, 295, 320, 416, 449, 453
Wheeler, Tolman & c. MA:299, 301

Whitacre, John MA:12

Whitaker & Adams JA:6
Whitaker, James
   JA:7
   MA:64
Whitaker, John
   CA:61, 63-67
   MA:25, 54
Whitaker, Wessel
   JA:62
   MA:320, 395, 443

White Pigeon CA:29, 31, 528
White, Albert L. MA:2

White, Asher MA:126
White, Peter
  CA:17, 417, 563
  MA:2, 28, 44, 498
White, Peter naturalization MA:10
White, Peter naturalization sig mark MA:9, 11

Whitehead, Herman [William crossed out] sig JA:171
Whitehead, John MA:382
Whitehead, William H. CA:500
Whitehead, William H. bail CA:499

Whitman, Julius CA:464

Whitmore, Julius
  CA:467, 495, 529, 541, 558, 563, 583
  MA:383

Whittaker & Adams
  CA:29
  MA:55
Whittaker, James
  CA:29, 31, 32
  MA:55, 65
Whittaker, John CA:173

Whittem, James MA:24, 302

Whitten, J. JA:125
Whitten, James JA:73
Whitten, James sig JA:113

Wick & Manning JA:37
Wick, Caleb B.
  CA:432
  JA:61
  MA:293, 438

Wickham, William D. M. JA:166

Wilber, Shepherd MA:320, 443

Wiles, Aaron JA:130, 195

Wilkerson, Joseph MA:323, 336, 353
Wilkerson, W. CA:321

Wilkinson, I. CA:548, 550
Wilkinson, James A. JA:190
Wilkinson, John W. JA:100
Wilkinson, John W. bail JA:47
Wilkinson, John W. bail sig MA:353
Wilkinson, Joseph N.
  JA:47, 71
  MA:313, 480, 481, 484

Wilkison, John W. bail CA:268
Wilkison, Joseph N. CA:267, 404, 406

Williams, Ebenezer L. JA:147
Williams, Herbert JA:145
Williams, Ludlow JA:127, 134, 172, 193

Williams, S. CA:540
Williams, Sidney [crossed out] MA:207
Williams, Sidney
   CA:379, 380, 530, 531, 533-535, 540, 541
   JA:37, 68, 69, 86, 94, 96, 98, 99, 103, 112, 115, 119, 194, 195
   MA:93, 110, 121, 216, 292, 468, 472, 526
Williams, Ulas MA:27
Williams, Uzal
   CA:24, 48
   JA:10
   MA:31, 33, 34, 39, 40, 42, 44, 53, 93
Williams, Washington [crossed out] MA:87
Williams, Washington JA:1, 8, 10, 17, 74, 90, 94

Willis, John
   CA:414, 462, 463
   MA:382, 396

Wills & Enos CA:515, 522, 523
Wills, David JA:173
Wills, J. R. CA:308, 309
Wills, James MA:418
Wills, John JA:173, 174

Willys, John CA:460

Wilson, Adam JA:152
Wilson, Daniel JA:101
Wilson, Daniel M. [crossed out] MA:216

Wilson, Daniel M.
 JA:44
 MA:221
Wilson, Daniel M. & c. MA:339
Wilson, Jas JA:113
Wilson, Joshua JA:139, 144
Wilson, Walter [crossed out]
 JA:59
 MA:458
Wilson, Walter
 CA:43, 50, 237, 238, 347, 348, 358, 359
 JA:5, 7, 12, 35, 55, 63, 69
 MA:68, 71, 81, 114, 283, 380, 381, 426, 448, 461, 472
Wilson, William
 CA:462, 467, 495
 MA:383

Winchell, Lyman P. JA:143

Winchell/Winchel, Nathaniel MA:12, 25
Winchell, William B.
 JA:70
 MA:389, 478

Winchester, Daniel
 CA:269
 MA:311, 350
Winchester, Daniel sig JA:47

Windham County, Vermont CA:55
Windle, William
  CA:246
  JA:52

Winfrey, Wesley
  CA:111, 112
  MA:187, 262, 397

Wing, Joseph MA:442
Wing, Josiah
  CA:335, 393, 405, 410, 415, 421, 427, 430
  MA:437, 455, 461, 480, 485, 492, 502, 512, 515
Wing, Josiah W. MA:382

Wisconsin Territory CA:508, 509

Witherell, John B. JA:119

Witter, Crandall JA:184, 192

Wolcott, Levi JA:72

Wolverton, Charles JA:136

Wood, Johnson, & Barrett JA:177

Wood, Leonard JA:57

Wooden, Timothy   CA:143
    JA:22   MA:161

Woodruff, Asahel JA:148

Woods, Timothy sig MA:161

Woodson, E. B. MA:497
Woodson, Edmund B. JA:155
Woodson, Edmund B. JP CA:582

Woodward, Benjamin JA:108
Woodward, Benjamin JP
    CA:528, 529
    MA:380, 390, 393-395

Wortman, Milton JA:107

Wright, Alexander H. MA:488
Wright, Henry H. JA:113
Wright, James B. [crossed out] JA:113
Wright, James B. bail CA:573
Wright, Joseph MA:383
Wright, Willis G. JA:113

Wyatt, Joseph
 CA:529, 568
 JA:109, 184, 196Wyatt, Joseph estate JA:116
Wyatt, Joseph sig JA:117, 126

Wyten?, William CA:141 page attached

YZ

Yates, Chapman JP CA:528

Yellow River Road CA:428

Young, Henry JA:125
Young, Henry bail JA:126

Zabriskie, William MA:364

Zurey, William CA:323

www.ingramcontent.com/pod-product-compliance
Lightning Source LLC
Chambersburg PA
CBHW060123170426
43198CB00010B/1013